CHARLIE FLOWERS & THE MELODY GARDENS

CHARLIE FLOWERS & THE MELODY GARDENS

FRED HOWARD

LIVERIGHT · NEW YORK

Liveright Publishing
386 Park Avenue South, New York, New York 10016

1.987654321
International Standard Book Number: 0-87140-555-5
Library of Congress Catalog Card Number: 72-78409

Manufactured in the United States of America
Designed by The Etheredges

CHARLIE FLOWERS & THE MELODY GARDENS

ONE

The best place to begin a story is at the beginning and the beginning is in Chicago where I was born. My father's name was Henry Flowers and my mother's name was Isabel Flowers and they had a song and dance act back in the days of the First World War when vaudeville was not as dead as vaudeville is now. When I came along my name turned out to be Charlie Flowers. It wasn't long before my father changed the name of the act from The Two Flowers to The Three Flowers and stuck me into it. I can still remember that act—my mother singing and rolling her eyes around in the dusty spotlight, my father cranking a fake barrel organ and bellowing "O Sole Mio" at the top of his lungs, and myself in a velvet monkey suit attached to the barrel organ by a long chain, dancing and turning somersaults and pulling my cap off and putting it on again.

I don't remember my mother very well. There is a half-developed picture floating around in my mind of my mother holding me between her knees and putting some lines on my face with an orange stick, saying "Be still, monkey." Her eyes were big and beautiful but the pupils were so large they made her look almost cross-eyed. Another time I remember her bending over me in a hotel bedroom, her dark hair falling against my cheek. There was an old-fashioned gas jet over the bed. It was unlit but going full blast. "Are you crazy, Isabel?" I heard my father shouting. "Are you trying to kill the boy?"

Not long after that we moved into my grandmother's house on the North Side in Chicago. That was my mother's mother and her name was Amanda Slaughter. She kept half a dozen boarders and fed them two meals a day, so her kitchen was a big one and so was the stove. One night when I was four years old, my mother rocked me to sleep in the dark kitchen in front of the stove. The oven door was open. The burners were unlit and there was the same smell of escaping gas as that other time but the hissing was louder. Suddenly the light went on and the kitchen filled up with people.

I wasn't allowed to see my mother until after supper the next night when I was dressed up and led into the parlor to say good-bye. She took me in her arms and stared at me kind of pleasant with her big dark eyes. Even now

I'm not sure she wasn't a little cross-eyed. When my grandmother tried to separate us I began to holler.

"Let the boy alone," said my father. "He can go along in the taxi."

"That'll cost extra," said my grandmother.

"I want to go in the taxi," I hollered.

I went in the taxi. I sat on the little seat facing my mother and father and wondered where we were going. The taxi followed the streetcar tracks until they came to an end, then it went under an arch and stopped in front of a red brick building. It had a high porch with an electric light in the middle of it. My father started up the steps with the suitcase. When it dawned on me what was happening I shouted, "Don't go!" and gave my mother's skirt such a yank she almost fell over backwards. Her dress must have been made of wool because I can still feel it in my hands when I think of it.

"Don't make a fuss, Isabel," said my father. "You'll see the boy in a week or two."

My mother didn't make a fuss. She just looked down at me sort of foolish and said, "Why, Henry, what's the matter with the little monkey?"

My father took me back to my grandmother's house in the taxi and I was put to bed on the couch in the dining room. I lay staring up at the plate rail, holding back the few tears I had left while Minnie, the deaf-and-dumb hunchback who did my grandmother's housework, brought in a pot of coffee and set it on the table between my father and my grandmother. My grandmother poured two cups of coffee and said, "You can't leave him with me, Henry Flowers."

"Now Amanda, not in front of the boy. It's just until I get back on my feet."

I turned my face to the wall and closed my eyes so they wouldn't know I was listening. I was afraid I would never see my mother again and I wanted to die. When I finally did go to sleep, I didn't want to ever wake up again, not in this world. But I did. Either that, or I have been dreaming a long time and will wake up any minute now to see Minnie shuffling in to set the table for the boarders' breakfast while the sun comes pouring over the wall of the Melody Gardens into the dining room of my grandmother's house next door.

The Melody Gardens were a Chicago showplace in those days. The main entrance, on my grandmother's street, was built like a row of castles with towers and gables all painted white so when the colored lights were turned on after dark they looked like they were glowing with rainbow colors inside. The kitchen of the Melody Gardens extended as far back as our dining room. A whitewashed wall ran across the block from there, cutting it in half, and a wooden fence ran around the Gardens the rest of the way. From the sidewalk, looking in through the knotholes in that fence, you could get good glimpses of the open-air beer garden and the bandstand and the little stage. Tall trees rustled above the tables. Japanese lanterns hung from electric wires between the trees and swayed in the breeze that smelled of Lake Michigan only three blocks away. After dark, when the lanterns were lit, waiters ran up and down the gravel paths with napkins over their arms. The band played until midnight in the summertime. You could hear it all over the block.

My grandmother's house, being right next door, is all mixed up with the Melody Gardens in my mind. It was nice enough in the summer with the music pouring over the high brick wall but I remember it best like it was in the winter when the whitewashed wall was gray with soot and the outdoor gardens were closed for the season—a plain old-fashioned house with high ceilings and an attic. There was a pedestal in the parlor with a fern on it and a jar of dried rose petals on the mantel. Next to the jar was a bottle with a sailing boat inside. The boat had been made by my grandfather who had long white whiskers. He put the boat in the bottle, a few pieces at a time, then he died.

There was a large bookcase in the parlor. One day not long after I went to live with my grandmother, she caught me playing with the books. The books must have belonged to my grandfather because she took them away from me and locked the shiny glass doors of the bookcase and put the key in the jar of dried rose petals on the mantel. "Never touch the books," she said. "It might disturb your grandfather." After that I avoided the bookcase as much as possible. I was sure that if I climbed on a chair and looked behind the books on the top shelf I would see a dead man with a long white beard.

The boarders were women mostly. They were all unmarried or looked as if they wanted to be. I didn't care for any of them but the person I liked least in that house was Minnie, the deaf and dumb hunchback. Minnie was like a slave to my grandmother. Her knuckles were the size of small onions and her face was covered with tiny brown splotches that couldn't have been freckles because Minnie never went out in the sun like other people except to empty the garbage.

One day when I had been living in that house for about a year, my grandmother took me aside and said, "I have something to tell you, Charlie. Your mother is dead." I still think a look of satisfaction came into her face when I began to bawl, but if it did the joke was on my grandmother. I wasn't afraid of not having a mother any more. I was already used to that. I was afraid they would bring her home and stuff her behind the books in the bookcase and she would lie there forever, like my grandfather, with her hands crossed on her stomach.

It was like I feared. Two days later the shades were pulled down in the parlor and my mother was laid out in a coffin next to the fern. My father showed up for the funeral. So did all the boarders. Pastor Froelich, a good friend of my dead grandfather's, made a speech and everybody sang a hymn. Then my father lifted me up to look at my mother. "Now go upstairs and take a good nap," he said. But I couldn't sleep. In my mind's eye I could see my father and Pastor Froelich lifting my mother out of the coffin and stuffing her behind the books in the bookcase and my grandmother locking the glass doors and putting the key in the jar of dried rose petals on the mantel.

But my mother wasn't buried in the bookcase after all. The next day my father took me to the cemetery and showed me her grave on a little hill beside the elevated tracks. There were some yellow roses in a can of water on top of it. My father snapped two of them off at the stem.

He put one in his buttonhole and gave the other to me. "Now show me grandpa's grave," I said.

"Your grandfather doesn't have a grave. He used to be on the mantel but your grandmother is always moving him around. Where do you suppose she put the old bastard now?"

"Is the bastard in the old bookcase?" I suggested. Just then an elevated train went screeching by. I couldn't hear a word my father said. "What?" I shouted.

"I say," shouted my father, "watch your language, boy."

Then he took my hand and I walked back to the elevated station beside him, smelling the yellow rose and wondering how I was ever going to find my way back to that magic land of spotlights and fake barrel organs and monkey suits where we had all been so happy together.

The arguments between my father and my grandmother began the day after the funeral and lasted all summer. They began when my father discovered I was still sleeping in the dining room.

"That's no fit place for the boy to sleep."

"Where did you expect him to sleep? The best room in the house?"

"I can't afford a larger room now but as soon as I get a job—"

"When you get a job will be plenty of time to talk about that. With God's help you might be able to take him off my hands."

My father didn't like to walk any more than I did but we walked for miles that summer, just to get away from my grandmother. Generally we wound up in Finkel's Pharmacy near the elevated station for a glass of grape juice. My grandmother had a charge account there and my father talked Mr. Finkel into putting the grape juice on my grandmother's bill. Once a week we went to the Victoria.

The Victoria was the best vaudeville house on the North Side. The seats were large and comfortable and had little metal tags on the back of them. The ticket taker let us in for nothing. Professional courtesy, my father said. "The Pendexters are here this week," said the ticket taker. "You remember the Pendexters, Mr. Flowers?"

"Do I remember the Pendexters! Greatest bellringers in the business."

Every Friday night they had a serial at the Victoria. After the steel curtain went up, the lights would go out and a ghostly white movie screen would come slowly down and hit the stage with a bump. When the serial was over, a bell buzzed backstage, the footlights went on, and the vaudeville began. On the same bill as the Pendexters was a seal by the name of the Great Jake. It balanced a ball and blew a set of bugles with its nose. The Pendexters were almost as good as the seal. They ran around the stage, ringing everything in sight, bells, drinking glasses, bottles, even a chandelier.

When the serial came on again, we went backstage and visited Mr. and Mrs. Pendexter in their dressing room. Mrs. Pendexter blew her nose in a silk handkerchief when my father told her about my mother. Isabel had such beautiful eyes she said. "So this is Charlie," said Mr. Pendexter. "He looks more like a monkey than ever."

"He don't remember me," chimed in his wife. "I used

8

to hold him in my arms during his mamma's act. That was a fine act, Henry. I'll never understand why it didn't make the big time. What are you doing now?"

"You might say I'm in the brokerage business."

"Bonds and stocks and stuff! You ought to be ashamed of yourself. People always liked The Two Flowers."

"Three," said my father.

"Well, it's two now. Or it could be. Essie Jones has both kids with her since Sam died."

I was in second heaven that night. Here were the best bellringers in the business paying more attention to me than anybody ever paid to me in my grandmother's house. Here was Mrs. Pendexter leading me across the dark stage behind the big movie screen to meet the seal. She took me into a bathroom and there was Jake with his chin on the edge of the bathtub. "Shake hands," she said. "Shake hands with Charlie." On the way home we stopped in Finkel's Pharmacy for a glass of grape juice. Mr. Finkel looked at me through his thick glasses and said, "Such a big boy as you have, Mr. Flowers. I wish I had a big boy like him." I was sleepy but I was still in second heaven. "I shook hands with Jake," I said. "I shook hands with a seal."

It wasn't long before my father began to talk of going back on the stage and taking me with him. "You fill that boy's head with that kind of talk and he'll wind up like his poor mother," said my grandmother. She didn't have any more use for my father than she did for the stage but she thought it would be a good way to get rid of us both at one crack so she let us clear out a space next to the furnace room in the basement where we could work on the act.

I don't imagine many kids would have ambitions to go

on the stage at the age of five except a few girls maybe, but my head was so full of the vaudeville at the Victoria I couldn't get enough of it. The new act was mostly one long monologue by my father but there were a couple of songs in it and a little patter to cement the dances together. My father taught me a buck-and-wing and we did a cakewalk, using canes made out of broomsticks, a long one for him and a short one for me. When we got to the end of the act we would clap and shout bravo. Then we would come running out from behind the coalbin, taking bow after bow, as if we were already on the stage at the Victoria in front of the curtain with all the advertisements on it.

One afternoon we went downtown to see a friend of my father's about a booking, but the inside of a theatrical agency was so different from my grandmother's basement I could no more remember what I was supposed to do than sing in grand opera. I began to cry and kept crying until my father took me out of that place. I recovered in time to go to the Victoria that night but my father's heart wasn't in it like mine was. He plunked me down in the third row and told me to wait until he got back. That was the Friday the girl in the serial got shoved off the cliff. The last I saw of her she was hanging over the edge of the canyon in her cowgirl outfit, clawing at a rock that was giving way a little at a time. During the second show I fell asleep.

When I woke up an usher was shaking me and the theater was empty. An electric light without any shade on it hung over the orchestra pit. There were Cracker Jack boxes in the aisles. The seats looked dirty and threadbare.

"It's Hank Flowers' boy," said the usher to the ticket taker.

They couldn't find my father anywhere so the usher took me home. We got as far as the Melody Gardens, then he turned me over to the doorman in the long green coat who knew where I lived and he took me the rest of the way.

"Like father, like son," said my grandmother when she opened the door. "From now on, there'll be no more dancing and prancing and stirring up coal dust in the basement. Anybody living in this house is going to work for his supper, not dance for it."

My grandmother never had any trouble getting boarders. The day after my father left, she put a sign in the window and the day after she put the sign in the window she got Mabel. As soon as my grandmother opened the door Mabel stuck her foot in it. "Now I'll be frank with you," she said. "I haven't a cent in the world and the only clothes I have are on my back but I saw that sign in your window and I'd like to rent that room."

It wasn't any time at all before Mabel was in the kitchen, drinking coffee and pouring out her troubles to my grandmother. She was a piano player in a movie house on Sheridan Road. Only the other day a man was going to marry her, she said, so she gave him all her money to rent a flat with and he never came back. Then her landlady threw her out and kept all her clothes because she owed two weeks' rent. But she did have property. She had a piano, a lovely piano, only it was in storage and she couldn't get it out because she didn't have any money.

Whenever my grandmother started to talk about the rent, Mabel changed the subject. She knew just the place for her piano she said, the little alcove at the end of the hallway next to the dining room where it wouldn't be in anybody's way. Because just as soon as she got enough money together she was going to have it taken out of storage. And of course she did have a job and her credit was good, wasn't it, especially with all that property, even if it was in storage.

Mabel not only talked my grandmother into renting her the room but into loaning her enough money to get back on her feet. Two weeks later she paid my grandmother back every penny she borrowed and after that the way my grandmother talked about Mabel you would have thought Mabel was made of gold. There was something golden about her. She wore her hair in braids twisted around the top of her head. Loose ends of hair floated around her ears like golden fuzz. She took a shine to me and let me wander around her room while she was dressing and pick up the long braid on the dresser and hold it in my hands. When I asked her what she called it, she said "My crowning glory." Crowning glory! I thought that was wonderful. Mabel could take off her hair just like other people took off their underwear and put it on again after a bath.

One day the movers came with Mabel's piano and put it in the alcove next to the dining room just like she said they would. Nights when she wasn't working she played it after dinner. Sometimes she sang. When she held a high note her voice trembled up and down over the note as if she was hugging and kissing it and would never let it go.

Except for Mabel's coming to live with us, things went along that year as usual until Minnie fell down the basement steps. A week later she died in County Hospital. Kids are funny. All my life I hated Minnie but as soon as she was dead she became the best friend I had in the world. I missed her long arms and spotted face and hunched-up back. I was thankful for Minnie's sake they never brought her back and put her in the bookcase.

After Minnie died, a German lady moved in to help my grandmother with the housework. First she refused to sleep on the back porch because it was too cold, then she refused to take care of the furnace, then she quit. Then a Negro lady came in by the day. Her name was Delilah and she was always talking about the devil. Before the winter was over my grandmother fired Delilah and started doing all the work herself. I was almost seven by then. "The least you can do is help around the house," said my grandmother. "Your father's not paying me a penny for your keep." I began by emptying wastebaskets and graduated to a dust-pan and a broom. Then I learned to wash dishes sitting on a high stool.

As luck would have it, Mabel lost her job that spring. She came home one night and threw herself on my grand-mother's shoulder. The movie house where she worked had installed an organ and Mabel didn't know how to play the organ. She didn't know what she was going to do. She would have to sell her piano to live.

There, there, said my grandmother, she was not to worry. She could help with the housework until she found another job. She rented out Mabel's room and fixed Mabel a place in the attic to sleep. Mabel said my grandmother was so kind to her she would play the piano for the boarders during meals for nothing. That was about all she did. The way it turned out, I helped with the housework while

Mabel sat around the kitchen all day in an old purple petticoat, talking and drinking coffee with my grandmother until it was time for dinner. Then she put on her crowning glory and sat down at the piano in the alcove off the dining room and played soft music while the boarders sipped their soup and wondered what had happened to my grandmother's mind.

One night at the beginning of summer, Mabel had just got up from the piano and gone in the kitchen to get a drink of water when my father walked in. He was a changed man. His stomach stuck out farther than before but his clothes were pressed and he smelled like a barber shop. "Good evening, Amanda," he said, kissing my grandmother on the cheek. "Hello, boy," he added, running his hand through my hair like an afterthought.

"We will proceed with the dinner," said my grandmother. "You may wait in the parlor." After dinner she washed my face with a dishcloth that smelled of onion, then we went in the parlor and I climbed on my father's knee and glared at my grandmother.

"I'm taking the boy off your hands, Amanda. We're leaving for Colorado in the morning. I'm in the mining business now. Gold mining," he said, turning a ring around on his finger and polishing it and holding it up to the light. "We're still in the promoting stage. Not that we need any more capital, but if you could spare a penny or two, you couldn't make a safer investment."

"Absolutely not. You know, Henry, it isn't as though Charlie was a boarder here. He's my grandson. I've worked hard to support him since his mother died. I have a claim on him too."

"I understand, Amanda. After all he is your heir."

"My what? Why Henry Flowers, every penny that comes into this house goes back into food and linen. I can't even afford a maid. If it wasn't for Mabel I don't know what I'd do. Look here," she went on more cheerful, "you and Charlie can have the big bed in my room and I'll sleep in the dining room. You can stay as long as you like."

It was my father's turn to look surprised. "We'll talk about it in the morning," he said. "How's school, boy?"

"They wouldn't accept him last term. Politics," said my grandmother. "The Republicans."

Mabel suddenly appeared in the doorway, her yellow braids glowing like the halo on an angel. "Am I interrupting, Amanda dear? I didn't want you to worry about the dishes. I'll take care of them. Maybe Charlie will help me dry."

"I'll dry," said my grandmother. "I want to talk to you about something, Mabel." They went in the kitchen. My father coughed.

"Who's that?"

"That's Mabel," I said.

My grandmother talked my father into staying longer than he intended. I didn't mind because I got to sleep in the best room in the house and didn't have to help with the housework any more. Mabel did more than her share, singing like a lark all over the house by day and playing the piano very loud at night for my father's benefit.

When the Fourth of July came around my father brought home a big box of fireworks. After dark the boarders stood around the backyard holding sparklers and Roman candles while my father nailed pinwheels to the clothes-poles and set them off and my grandmother ran around stamping out sparks and the music from the Melody Gardens floated over the whitewashed wall like music in a dream. "Mr. Flowers," whispered Mabel when the fireworks were over, "would you mind if I took Charlie up to the attic? My little window is just big enough for the two of us. We can watch the skyrockets from Cubs Park and hug each other just like this."

My father coughed.

"Maybe we should let your daddy come too," said Mabel.

I had never been in the attic before. A half-dead tree that my grandmother always meant to have cut down came right up to the window in Mabel's room, blocking the Melody Gardens, but on the other side you could see clear over to Cubs Ballpark. Mabel said the room was just right for her. It was nice of my grandmother to let her live there like the little church mouse she was. So my father put an arm around me and Mabel put an arm around me and I watched the skyrockets bursting over the ballpark until I fell asleep.

We went everywhere that summer. We went downtown to the old Palace on Clark Street where there were no movies, only vaudeville, and it was even better than the Victoria. We went to Riverview where the roller coasters were and my father let me stuff myself with cotton candy and ride the Shoot-the-Chutes. Mabel met us there for dinner. The Chutes were too high for Mabel so we went on The Thousand Islands, a boat ride they had at the time. The boat floated through tunnels and between cardboard mountains and went barging down a rapids. My father sat in back with Mabel so I could have a seat to myself. When we came out of the tunnel I turned around. A hairpin was sticking out of Mabel's braids and she was putting it back in. "Goodness," said Mabel, "I never saw such a man. I mean such a nice man."

The summer wore on. My grandmother kept saying, "Take your time, Henry. I'll hate to see Charlie go." Finally my father couldn't put it off any longer. He bought two tickets to Denver and the day before the train left we went to the circus to celebrate. We had dinner downtown. My grandmother was at the movies when we got home so Mabel let us in and put me to bed but I couldn't sleep, what with the Cracker Jack waltzing around in my stomach and the clowns in my head. Finally I heard a noise in the hall and opened the door.

My grandmother and a policeman were standing in front of the attic door at the end of the hall. All at once there was a scream in the attic. "Now!" said my grandmother, and the policeman started up the steps.

There was a sound of scuffling and of something heavy being pushed downstairs. The first thing that popped in my head was that a bear had escaped from the circus and was eating Mabel up, but when the policeman came through the door, it wasn't a bear he had by the collar, it was my father. Mabel followed right behind. She was in her bathrobe and her hair was streaming down her back.

"You gonna prefer charges?" said the policeman.

"I don't think that will be necessary," said my grandmother.

My father shook himself free and ran into our room,

picking me up on the way like a sack of mail. Fifteen minutes later we were packed and ready to go.

My grandmother was standing at the front door with her arms folded.

"You've caused enough trouble in this house, Henry. I'll thank you to go quietly and not wake the boarders. Charlie stays with me."

"He goes with me."

"Do you think any court in the country would award you custody of the child after what's happened tonight? Who would you use for character witness? Mabel?"

"Oh the brute," said Mabel, stepping out from behind the fern in the parlor. "He attacked me."

"Get that old whore out of my sight," roared my father and dashed out the door. We could hear him halfway to the elevated station, bellowing threats and curses against Mabel and my grandmother, all mixed up with promises to come back and take me away. He left for Colorado the next day and we never saw him again.

TWO

I began school that year. I was the biggest, dumbest boy in the first grade and just about the shabbiest. "Doesn't your mother ever take care of you?" said the teacher.

"He doesn't have a mother," said a little girl by the name of Dolly who lived in our block. "He has a grandmother."

It was a mystery at first why I hadn't been allowed to go away with my father. By the time it dawned on me, it was too late. I had already become a second Minnie to my grandmother. I grew up thinking it was natural to dry dishes without breaking them, thinking it was natural to mop under the boarders' beds every day after school and to scrub the kitchen linoleum and clean the toilet bowl on Saturdays. By the time I was eight I was making beds, by the time I was nine I could iron. "What a help to you the boy is," said the boarders.

"Well," said my grandmother, "I can't do it all by myself, what with my gallstones and all."

My grandmother didn't even have gallstones until Mabel came along. When the attic got too cold for her, Mabel got herself a job playing the piano in a small movie house on Clark Street and moved into her old room. She spent more time than ever drinking coffee in the kitchen and discussing diseases. She had the idea my grandmother was sick and ought to go to the doctor's before it was too late, she might have cancer or something. So my grandmother started going to the doctor's. When she came home they talked over what the doctor said and came to the conclusion that my grandmother should have her gallstones out only she never had the time. She would send me over to Finkel's Pharmacy with a prescription instead.

"So your grandmother gave you the money this time?"

"She said to charge it."

"Charge it, always charge it. Your grandmother thinks I am made of gold? She thinks I am in business for her benefit? Go on, go on," said Mr. Finkel. "What do you want for nothing now?"

"A penny bottle."

"They cost money."

"Charge it."

Mr. Finkel would reach in the penny candy case and

take out one of the little paraffin bottles filled with syrup. After drinking the syrup you could chew the empty bottle until your jaws ached. I was chewing one the day I met Stinko.

Stinko lived in one of the apartment houses behind the Melody Gardens but I never spoke to him until the day he came into Finkel's and rapped on the counter with a penny. "Who waits to the penny candy?" he shouted. When Mr. Finkel came out of the back room, Stinko said, "Give me a bottle a that, you big sheeny." Mr. Finkel gave him the bottle and chased us both out and we stood on the curb and looked at each other. Stinko bit the top off his bottle."That's a way you got to treat the sheenies."

"What's a sheeny?" I said.

"A sheeny is a guy when he gets hold of a baby boy he cuts his thing off."

"What thing?"

"This thing," shouted Stinko grabbing himself by the pants.

Stinko knew everything about everything. It was hard to know something he didn't know. One day I told him my grandfather was buried in the bookcase. He said he never heard anything like that before, he would like to see it. So next time my grandmother went downtown I let him in the house and we got the key out of the rose petal jar on the mantel and opened the glass doors to the bookcase. All we found was a red marble box about eight inches square with gold edges and a word in gold on the front of it. After all those years I was disappointed to find that my grandfather wasn't in the bookcase but I wouldn't let on.

"Is your grandfather in the box?" said Stinko.

"Sure," I said.

"How did he get to be so small?"

"I can't tell you," I said. "It's a family secret."

We put the key back in the jar of rose petals and took the marble box out in the backyard and tried to pry it open with an old crowbar. It wouldn't pry so Stinko gave it a powerful wham. The word in gold flew off and some gray powder came swirling out. We dropped the box like a hot potato and ran under the back porch.

"Was that your grandfather?" whispered Stinko.

"Who did you think it was?" I said. "The King of Siam?"

We decided we ought to bury him for good so we dug a hole under the elephant ears next to the wall of the Melody Gardens but it wasn't deep enough so we sprinkled dirt and dead leaves on the pile and trampled down the edges so it wouldn't show. Elephant ears was what we called the big-leaf plants that grew in my grandmother's backyard. If you ate a piece of a leaf you were supposed to die before sundown, only you never did.

The elephant ears got quite large that summer. When September came, they drooped lower and lower until they covered the dead leaves and the earth. About that time Mabel got after my grandmother to have the tree in the backyard cut down. She said it was half-dead, something ought to be done about it before it fell on the house. So my grandmother had it cut down. She stayed out in the back-yard the whole time to see the men didn't bash in the attic window. As it was, she claimed they ruined her snowball bushes and made them promise to come back and clean up the yard. When I got home from school the next afternoon the yard was raked clean as a whistle and there was a pile of dead leaves and rubbish burning in the middle of it. The first thing I saw when I went in the house was the marble box, lying on a newspaper on the kitchen table. My grandmother pointed to the box.

"Those are your grandfather's ashes. Do you know what happens to people who disturb the dead? They burn in hell."

"I didn't do it," I said. "I don't want to burn."

"Don't lie. I have half a mind to call Pastor Froelich," said my grandmother, starting for the telephone. I didn't know what Pastor Froelich had to do with it, but I could already feel the flames licking over me and the pitchforks sticking into me. I wasn't even sure what I'd done except that even if I hadn't done anything I had lied about it and would probably burn in hell anyway.

"Don't call him," I sobbed. "I did it."

My grandmother grabbed my hand and dragged me upstairs. "Up you go," she said when we came to the attic stairs, "and you don't come down until you say you're sorry." She slammed the door and turned the key.

"I'm sorry, I'm sorry," I screamed. I scratched and banged on the attic door but nothing happened. Finally I dragged myself up the steps to Mabel's old cot by the window where I lay down and cried until I fell asleep.

When I woke up it was dark. I could hear singing and laughing and music and applause. I thought at first I was dreaming and was back on the stage in the monkey suit. But I wasn't. Finally my curiosity got the better of me. I pulled myself up to the window and looked out.

For a minute I couldn't believe my eyes. Three stories

below lay the Melody Gardens, twinkling with a million lights, so beautiful and so close, now that the big tree was gone, I could almost reach out and touch them. I could see the people sitting at the little tables, I could see the chorus girls prancing down the runway, I could see the dancers, I could see the bandstand, I could see the band. I could see the whole show from beginning to end. It must have been after midnight when they turned off the lights in the lanterns between the trees. When I went to sleep a few seconds later, I had made up my mind what I was going to do with my life. I was going to follow in my father's footsteps. I was going back on the stage.

On winter evenings during those years, when it was already dark but not yet time for dinner, and smells of pork chops and fried potatoes came floating out of the areaways between the apartment buildings in our block, I would almost die of lonesomeness for the vaudeville at the old Victoria. Once a week Mabel would get the ticket taker in the little movie house on Clark Street to let me in for nothing. I can still see her, enthroned in the little light above the piano that was just bright enough to light up her face and braids, banging away at the keyboard and watching the screen at the same time. But the movies were only a substitute. One Saturday that spring we put on a show in Dolly's basement, using a sheet for a curtain. Dolly took dancing lessons, so she did a dance and then I did a dance. Another girl in our block sang a song and I tried to teach Stinko a cakewalk but he said dancing was for girls and pretended to make a stray dog do tricks. It was very good only Dolly's mother came downstairs and wanted her sheet back and nobody came anyway.

Aside from that there wasn't much I could do about going on the stage except listen to the band at the Melody Gardens in the summertime and watch the show and dream. My grandmother made me sleep in the attic regular now. There was no heat in the attic and I almost froze but there was no other place to sleep. My grandmother had rented out her old room and was sleeping on the couch in the dining room herself. Then there was one more roomer than before and more work than ever.

By my tenth birthday I was taking care of the furnace. My hands cracked and coal dust got in the cracks. At school I kept my hands in my pockets. I had a new teacher that year. She said Dolly told her I was doing janitor work and she was going to call on my grandmother, but when she came, my grandmother wouldn't answer the doorbell. "I have my hands full without talking to teachers," she said.

"You sure have," said Mabel, "you poor dear."

When school let out in June my grandmother went to the hospital to have her gallstones out. I stayed home and did the housework while Mabel collected the rents and listened to the boarders complain because they had to eat out. It wasn't long before two of them left. "Good riddance of bad garbage," said Mabel. I didn't give a damn either.

When my grandmother got back from the hospital she went right to bed. "I've stood by you all these years," she said, patting my hand. "Now you must stand by me. I'm going to rest for a few days. You and Mabel carry on as if I was still in the hospital."

She rested for a few days, then a few more days. The

days stretched themselves into weeks and the weeks stretched themselves into months while my grandmother went on resting and resting and the bills mounted up. When school opened in September she managed to drag herself out of bed and putter around the kitchen but she never again served meals to the boarders.

As far as school went, I was just as dumb in fourth grade as I was in third. The only thing I enjoyed was once a week when we had a class in the study of downtown Chicago. There was a map of the Loop in yellow chalk on the blackboard, showing the street names and where the important buildings were. Once a month we were supposed to go downtown with our parents' permission and visit the buildings. I never dreamed my grandmother would let me go but when I asked her she said, "Fine. You can pick up some eggs downtown. They're cheaper there." So every Friday after school I would go downtown and buy the cheapest cold-storage eggs in the basement of Hillman's department store and a couple of pounds of coffee special at the Boston Store and a slab of bacon in the food department of the Fair whenever they had a sale. Then I would walk down to the river and see how Wacker Drive was coming along and what new skyscraper went up that week.

When Christmas came around my grandmother said she would give me a present she saw advertised, some cowboy gloves with big cuffs on them like all the kids were wearing that winter. She gave me a dollar and told me I could pick out a pair when I went downtown to get the eggs. So I did. The gloves felt pretty good when I tried them on. I threw my old mittens in a trash can and started home with the eggs.

When I got off the elevated I heard bells clanging and smelled smoke. Mr. Finkel was outside the drugstore, blowing steam and wringing his hands. "It's the Melody Gardens," he said. "They're burning down."

There was a crowd half a block long in front of my grandmother's house. Stinko was being chased around the edge of it by a fireman. The fireman tripped over a hose and Stinko dived into the crowd. I plowed in after him and we wormed our way up to the rope. "What happened?" I said.

"Holy Christ, I thought you were kilt. There was a grease fire in the Melody kitchen. They put it out but the sparks set fire to your roof."

Sure enough, the whole attic was in flames. The firemen were pouring barrels of water into it and the rafters were standing out against the sky like old bones. But the house didn't burn down, not below the second story anyway. The roomers rescued what they could and went to hotels. At eleven o'clock the firemen pulled out and left Mabel and me and my grandmother huddled around a candle in the kitchen. Water was dripping everywhere like in a cave. A neighbor brought over a pot of hot coffee and set it on the cold stove. Mabel poured my grandmother a cup but my grandmother just stared at it, thinking and thinking. Finally she began to cry. Mabel tiptoed out in the hall and sat down at the piano that smelled of woodsmoke like everything else in that house and began to play. The piano had a ghostly sound in the half-burned house. Suddenly I reached up and touched Mabel's hair.

"Oh, Mabel, your braids! Are they safe?"

Mabel's only answer was to throw her arms around my neck and burst into tears. Her crowning glory was gone.

We went back in the kitchen and my grandmother opened her arms and I ran into them and started to bawl. The three of us cried for fifteen minutes like a three-piece statue in the middle of a fountain and when we got through we all felt a hundred percent better. I asked if I could have a cup of coffee and my grandmother said certainly, I was eleven years old, wasn't I? "He's a man now," said Mabel. "He'll have to take care of his grandmother in her old age."

"And he will too," snapped my grandmother.

I blushed and wiped my nose on my new gloves.

THREE

After the fire they tore down what was left of my grand-mother's house and we moved into the second floor of a two-flat building on Wilton Avenue, three blocks from the Melody Gardens. The back porch was so close to the elevated tracks that every time a train went by it felt like the cars were going through the middle of the kitchen and the passengers were looking down your throat to see what you had for breakfast. The dining room was crowded so I slept on a cot next to the kitchen window where I could sit up at night and see the people going by in the elevated trains without being seen by them. Mabel and her piano moved right along with us. The piano was never the same again. Neither was Mabel without her braids but she bought some hair puffs to take their place and with those two knobs of hair sticking out on either side of her head she looked almost as stylish as before.

Not long after the fire Pastor Froelich paid us a visit. If the old house burned down, even partway, he said, it was my grandmother's fault for not going to church since Grandfather Slaughter died. My grandmother guessed he was right but her health had failed and there was nothing she could do about it now. "You could send Charlie," boomed Pastor Froelich. "We have a fine Sunday school in the basement."

So every Sunday for a long time after that I shined my shoes and trooped off to Sunday school with ten cents in my pocket for the collection and a nickel for the missionary society. The church had a big basement where the Boy Scouts met every Friday night. Stinko joined the Boy Scouts when he got to be twelve but he was two months older than me and by the time I was old enough to join he had already got himself quite a reputation for breaking up meetings and talking dirty about girls. When I got to be twelve I wanted to join too. My grandmother said she was sorry but she couldn't see her way clear to buy me a uniform, not to mention the other stuff I would need like compasses and jackknives. I damn near cried. "Why you poor kid," said Mabel.

"He'll get over it," said my grandmother.

That night I decided it was time to cash in on the fifteen cents I was handing over to the Sunday school every week so I sat up in bed while the elevated trains went banging by the kitchen window and prayed God to send me a complete Boy Scout outfit. I didn't expect results right off but the very next morning Mabel told my grandmother she was going to take me downtown to carry some packages for her. We met a man in the waiting room at the Boston Store whose name was Herman and he took me upstairs and bought me a uniform. Mabel made me promise to tell my grandmother she paid for the uniform herself. I didn't mind. It was my last chance to tell a lie before I joined the Boy Scouts.

For a while after I became a Boy Scout I was quite good. Not having so much housework to do in the new house, I had more time to think about religion. The more I thought about it the more I realized that religion could be just as exciting as seeing a movie where everyone went to pieces and ended up in a dope den in Chinatown where they never did anything anyway except blow smoke out of their lungs. Pastor Froelich was always ranting about how wicked it was to go to the theater where you were exposed to women who showed their naked thighs. None of the Boy Scouts were sure what a thigh was but we had a rough idea and when I thought how I used to watch the show at the Melody Gardens through the attic window of the boarding-house, I began to think the real reason my grandmother's house burned down was due to the fact she was harboring a sinner under her roof without knowing it and the sinner was me. I didn't want the new house to burn down so I even quit going to the movies.

Another thing I did that year was pray. I would lock myself in the bathroom and pray until my mind began to fold over on itself like a Parker House roll. I went so far as to tell my grandmother I wanted to know the truth about my mother because if my mother went to hell for being on the stage I wanted to pray for her. No, said my grandmother, my mother didn't go to hell for being on the stage, she went crazy from it instead. She said the best thing I could pray for would be to not go crazy myself because there was a good chance of it. So I prayed to save myself from going crazy and I prayed to make my grandmother well and I prayed for Mabel not to use too much rouge and lipstick so she could get into heaven if it ever became necessary. I even prayed for Stinko to stop talking dirty. I prayed for the Boy Scouts too.

One night after scout meeting we stopped in Finkel's Pharmacy for an Eskimo pie. It was summer and Dolly was sitting at the soda fountain, sucking a vanilla soda. Dolly not only took dancing lessons, she took elocution lessons at a school downtown. Everywhere she went she carried her dancing slippers around with her in a bag. "I suppose you just danced at the Melody Gardens," said Stinko, giving her slipper bag a poke.

"Of course not," said Dolly. "I wouldn't dance in that rundown old place if I was paid for it. Tonight I danced at the Chicago Children's Theater on the Navy Pier. I'm a member there. And if you don't believe me you can come down to the pier Wednesday afternoon and see for yourself."

Stinko didn't believe Dolly danced at the Navy Pier any more than he believed she danced at the Melody Gardens. Neither did I but we decided to kill two birds with one stone and find out. Stinko intended to become a sailor when he grew up. He was crazy about boats and figured if we went down to the Navy Pier on Wednesday we could check up on Dolly and take a ride on one of the boats at the same time. So Wednesday I wangled fifty cents out of my grandmother and we took the streetcar down to the pier.

The Navy Pier sticks out of Chicago's side into Lake Michigan for almost a mile. In those days the Grand Avenue streetcars went clanging down between the docks to a red brick building full of popcorn and hotdog counters at the very end. There was a cafeteria on the third floor where you could buy your lunch and eat it on the roof garden, or you could bring your lunch and eat it at one of the open-air picnic tables on the second floor that was sure to be covered with puddles of pop and pieces of leftover baloney. The excursion boats parked on either side of the promenade. In between was a crack-the-whip ride and a merry-go-round with a mechanical hurdy-gurdy. Beyond the promenade were two towers with gilded tops and between the towers was an auditorium, a giant dome of steel and glass with windows around the upper stories. Beyond the pier were the breakwaters and beyond the breakwaters was the lake with all kinds of boats on its surface in the summertime. Most of the pier was uncovered to the sky but covered or not it smelled from one end to the other like no place on this earth ever smelled, a combination of streetcars and sweat and hot dogs and boats and fresh water and people and fish.

The first thing we did when we got off the streetcar was buy two bags of popcorn. Then we went out on the promenade to look at the boats. The ones that went to Lincoln Park were small but the *Florida,* which went to

Jackson Park, was large and had a big steel rocker arm on top to work the paddle wheels. There was a man with a megaphone standing beside the gangplank. The boat left in ten minutes he said. Just time enough to look for Dolly we figured. We climbed the stairs under one of the towers and came out on the narrow walk that went around the top of the auditorium.

The windows opened inward up there, giving a fine view of the collapsible wooden seats, half-filled with women and children, and the steel girders that arched up from the marble floor and came to an end in a long skylight like the backbone of a turtle. The stage didn't have any scenery. It didn't even have a curtain. It was like the inside of an eggshell painted blue with a big American flag hanging down the middle of it. There was a show going on all right but either it wasn't very good or it was almost over because the audience kept getting up and walking out.

We finished our popcorn just as Dolly came marching out on the stage dressed in red white and blue like Columbia, leading a parade of about twenty children in costumes of different nationalities with flags over their shoulders. "Let's break it up," said Stinko. We went downstairs to the drinking fountain and came back with both popcorn bags full of water. Stinko twisted the neck of his bag and dropped it through the window. Dolly was holding a flag out over the audience and the audience was repeating the salute to the flag after her. "I pledge allegiance to the flag of the United States of America and to the republic for which it stands."

"Pulop," went Stinko's bag in back of the last row.

"One nation, indivisible, with liberty and justice—"

My bag had more water in it.

BANG!

The audience broke for the doors and the piano began to hammer out "The Star-Spangled Banner" the way they do on a ship that is going down at sea. We ran down the stairs like we were being chased by a dozen cops. Stinko slapped a quarter on the ticket booth next to the *Florida* and the lady tore him off a ticket. I was going to do the same when I suddenly remembered how good I had been all summer and my hand froze in my pocket.

"We shouldn't have done that, Stinko. Suppose the boat sinks. We'd go straight to hell."

"Oh for God sake, it won't sink."

It didn't look like it would. All the same I couldn't bring myself to follow Stinko up the gangplank. There wasn't anything in the catechism about throwing bags filled with water but I figured it probably came under the Ten Commandments. Everything else did. I turned around and trooped back to the auditorium.

"You're letting the flies in," said a gray-haired lady sitting next to one of the large glass doors near the stage. "Come in or stay out. Are you a member?"

"No ma'am."

"Name?"

"Charlie Flowers."

She wrote it down on a card.

"Don't let him get away, Mrs. Hennessy!" shouted another lady who came bearing down from the other side of the auditorium like a ship with all its sails unfurled. She was in white from head to foot except for a long blue scarf that was floating out behind her in the breeze. "How would you like to be Christopher Columbus next Wednesday?" she said, coming to a stop. "It's an easy part. You're the right size."

I didn't say anything. A fly settled on the lady's ankle. She swatted at it with a large black notebook she was carrying.

"You're a member, aren't you? If not, what are you doing here?"

"I threw that bag through the window. I came to confess."

"You might have killed someone. Either give your name and address to Mrs. Hennessy and show up for rehearsal Friday afternoon or I'll turn you over to the police. Keep an eye on him, Mrs. Hennessy, while he makes up his mind. And don't try to get away, young man. Mrs. Hennessy is a policewoman."

"Yes, Miss Ives," said Mrs. Hennessy, flexing her muscles under her dress.

The lady disappeared into a door in the wall. She came out on the stage a few seconds later and began talking to a bunch of kids sitting on the floor. I turned my back on the stage so Dolly wouldn't recognize me. Finally some workmen came in the door and began folding the collapsible chairs and sweeping the marble floor with big pusher brooms. In about ten minutes the lady came back.

"Well, did you make up your mind?"

"I didn't mean to throw that bag. Scout's honor! Stinko talked me into it."

"Goodness, is that a name? Well, never mind, don't cry about it. I haven't time to listen to your apologies. I've already given the part to Benny. Let him go, Mrs. Hennessy, and before you leave, tell the men to spray the auditorium Friday. The flies are getting out of hand." She barged off under full sail, her long blue scarf trailing behind.

I slunk out, feeling like two cents. The crack-the-whip ride on the promenade was full of screaming kids. So was the merry-go-round. The cymbals above the hurdy-gurdy banged against each other in the sun. But the *Florida* was gone.

After that I began to have my doubts about religion. The next Sunday my grandmother laid fifteen cents for Sunday school on the dining room table as usual.

"I'm not going," I said.

"What's the matter with the little minister?" said Mabel. "He used to be so religious."

I didn't say anything. My grandmother put the fifteen cents back in her purse and winked at Mabel. "Fifteen cents saved is fifteen cents earned," she said.

"You said it," said Mabel.

My grandmother finally grew tired of sitting around the house waiting to die. Mabel said she ought to find herself a hobby. She ought to go downtown to Dennison's and learn to make artificial flowers out of crepe paper, everybody else was doing it. So my grandmother went downtown and brought some crepe paper home with her and some wire stems and leaves and paste and in no time at all she was turning out yellow tea roses and blue paper cornflowers and red American Beauties by the dozen. For her birthday that year Mabel gave her a reading lamp with a metal stem on it that could be bent this way and that way like the neck of a snake. My grandmother would sit for hours in the dining room that was dark even in the daytime because the houses were so close together in that block, cutting and pasting artificial flowers together in the light of the little reading lamp.

If I wanted to earn a little pocket money, my grandmother said, and make her happy into the bargain, I could try selling some of her flowers from door to door afternoons after school. She put some tissue paper in the bottom of a market basket and filled the basket with bunches of assorted cornflowers and roses and sent me out on the street with the basket over my arm. I went to every back door in our block, going in and out of backyards by way of the alley under the elevated tracks. Ladies peered out of windows and shook their heads. One lady gave me a nickel. She thought I was begging I guess. I took the flowers back to my grandmother.

"I can't sell them."

"Of course you can't, not if you look down your nose at them. A little salesmanship, that's what you need."

The next afternoon she pulled an old stocking cap over my ears, cut some holes in my old cowboy gloves, and sent me to a neighborhood six blocks away where nobody would recognize me. I sold three bunches of flowers for fifty cents apiece. My grandmother was pleased. It wouldn't be any time at all before I'd be earning a commission she said. For the time being, all the money that came in would have to go back into capital.

By the time spring came and the little red tassels we called caterpillars dropped from the trees and covered the sidewalks, I had become quite a hot salesman. Whenever anyone answered my knock I would wipe my nose on my sleeve and suck in my cheeks like I was starving. Every now and then some poor lady with six children clinging to her apron invited me in for a cup of coffee and bought half a dozen tea roses to put in a mason jar on the mantel. But my commission never came through. "I don't want to work for nothing," I told my grandmother.

"Why Charlie Flowers! For years I've kept a roof over your head. If it wasn't for the rent Mabel pays for the front bedroom we'd have been on the street long ago. The least you can do is help sell my flowers."

"I'd sooner starve," I said.

It happened I flunked seventh grade that year. When vacation came around my grandmother said, "I'll make a deal with you. You can go to summer school or you can sell flowers." So I went on selling flowers.

That was the summer Dolly's mother got friendly with Stinko's mother across their back porch. She said Dolly was going to the children's theater on the Navy Pier again that summer. It was a wonderful place for children. It got them out of the house. That was all Stinko's mother needed. She made him go down to the pier with Dolly. Stinko had quit the Boy Scouts like me and was ripe and ready for something new. I would be damned if I would spend all my time selling flowers for nothing, so I went too.

A show was put on every Wednesday afternoon, composed of songs and dances and plays. Every Friday night there was a performance that began with a couple of numbers warmed over from Wednesday afternoon and the last half of the program would be put on by some singing or dancing school for the sake of the publicity. There was a costume room on the third floor behind the blue eggshell dome that covered the stage, full of cheesecloth and broken maypoles, where mothers who brought their kids to the pier three afternoons a week sat and sewed and argued about the parts their children got. There were plenty of girls Dolly's age who could do everything Dolly could do but there were only a handful of boys as old as Stinko and me so we had it all over Dolly when it came to getting good parts.

The first show we were in was a play about two Hindu magicians, Mumbo and Jumbo. We wore high turbans and sawed an elephant in half consisting of two boys in long underwear with a trunk made out of dirty flannel. Afterwards Miss Ives told us how wonderful we were. Lucy Ives was the lady in charge. She didn't have any more memory than a rabbit and had forgotten all about the time she tried to get me to be Christopher Columbus in exchange for not handing me over to the cops. When Stinko told her I used to be on the stage she became quite interested so I told her about The Three Flowers and the monkey suit. "Did you ever play the Palace?" she wanted to know.

"Oh sure, we played that too," I said. I told her my parents were dead and I was living with my grandmother until I could finish school. After that she held me up before the other children as a fine example of a professional entertainer who wasn't afraid to take small parts because they all contributed to his education. She was cracked on the subject of education.

My grandmother never did understand what went on down at that place. One Friday night she was still awake when I got home, working on some American Beauties under the little reading lamp at the dining room table. Whatever it was I was doing down at that smelly old pier with Stinko she didn't like it, she said. It would be lots better for my health if I spent more time in the open air, selling her flowers from door to door.

"Oh for God sake, I do sell them, every chance I get."

"Where did you pick that expression up? From one of your lady friends at the pier? Fine manners they teach you down at that place. Next week you're going out in the fresh air every afternoon and get rid of some of my flowers before they fall apart from old age."

"But if I work every afternoon I can't be in the pageant."

"Mornings then. If you're so high and mighty you can dictate to your grandmother, you'll go out and get a job. You'll pay your way from now on."

"I suppose I can pick a job off a tree."

"We'll cross that bridge when we come to it," said my grandmother.

Every summer there was a pageant at the pier to wind up the season. It was put on Wednesday afternoon and Friday night on the floor of the auditorium with the chairs ranged around the edge like a bullring, but the main performance took place Thursday in a place north of Chicago called Ravinia where they had an opera house and a ballpark. The pageant went on in the ballpark with real trees and a silver water tower for background. Boys and girls from all over the North Shore came with their mothers to eat popcorn in the grandstand, and a Chicago newspaper sent a trainload of poor kids up from the city on the North

Shore electric to sit in the grandstand next to the rich children and watch the pageant too.

The pageant that year was a Peace Pageant. It began in the Stone Age with some cavemen signing a treaty on a piece of rock after hitting each other over the heads with clubs. The next scene was a battle between some knights. Then they signed a peace treaty. The pageant also included the Battle of Bunker Hill and the Civil War and ended with President Wilson signing a final treaty of peace forever.

Stinko had four parts like me. Benny Hirschfield had three, including George Washington. In the grand finale, Benny was supposed to represent a soldier, Stinko a sailor, and me a marine. We were to lead the parade in review past President Wilson, a tall girl with a sour face, and Dolly, who was the Spirit of Peace. At the last minute Stinko had an idea. We tore up handkerchiefs and tied them around our arms and legs and heads and smeared lipstick on them like we were wounded. Just then Miss Ives sailed around the grandstand with a megaphone in her hand and stopped dead.

"You can't go on like that. This is a Peace Pageant."

"Then why the hell does it have so much fighting in it?" said Stinko.

Before Stinko knew what hit him, Miss Ives grabbed him by the arm and swung him around so his back hit the grandstand with a thud, knocking the wind out of him. "Don't ever, ever, use language like that in my presence, young man," she said.

Stinko was washed up for good. He didn't show up for the Friday night performance at the pier. Miss Ives gave two of his parts to me and one to Benny. We spent half the show changing costumes. When the spotlights were turned off and the red white and blue lights went on that covered each girder from the top of the auditorium to the bottom, I felt almost sorry the summer was over.

On my way up to the costume room with an armful of costumes I bumped into Lucy Ives on the stairs.

"I appreciate what you did tonight," she said. "I'm already making plans for next year. I'm keeping you in mind."

"I won't be back next summer."

"Oh! Are you planning to return to vaudeville?"

"It's not that," I said. "I'll be too old for this kid stuff next year."

"Kid stuff! My dear boy, if that's the way you feel about it, I wouldn't want you back under any circumstances." Then she laughed. "You have lots to learn," she said, flinging her long blue scarf over her shoulder. "Goodnight, Charles."

The little movie house on Clark Street switched from silent pictures to talking pictures that year and Mabel lost her job. Two weeks later she went to work for a jewelry firm as a collection agent, collecting money from people who bought diamonds and watches on time.

One day she brought home a little round handkerchief bag covered with cloth petals. She said one of her clients wanted a corsage made out of the same material. So my grandmother bought some remnants and sewed a corsage with silk petals and wire stems, tearing it apart three times until she got it right. Mabel's client showed it to a friend who ordered another just like it and a bag to match for five dollars. Mabel took the bag and corsage with her when she went to call on another client whose husband was a Mason. It turned out half of Mabel's clients bought rings and jewelry to wear to Masonic affairs and they all wanted handkerchief bags and corsages to go with them.

It wasn't long before the sideboard began to overflow with scraps of gold and silver cloth and red silk for petals and satin linings for the insides of handkerchief bags. My grandmother tried to get me to sell the stuff from door to door but I revolted. "None of my clients go to Masonic affairs," I said.

"Don't use that tone with me," she snapped. "It's been ten years since your father left. Ten years you've had to eat me out of house and home. If you're going to be so independent you'll pay me back every penny you owe or you won't eat. And that's final. Now run down to Finkel's and get my prescription refilled. The box is in the bathroom. Tell him to put it on the bill."

Finkel's Pharmacy hadn't changed much since the old days. Bottles of colored water still hung in the window. The chairs at the tables still had wire backs shaped like hearts. Mr. Finkel came out of the back room and looked at me through his thick glasses.

"Tell your grandmother to make a settlement on her bill. Then I will fill her prescription. When her house burned down I didn't bother her for money then. But yesterday Mrs. Jacobs comes in. She tells me your grandmother bought her old house from her with cash from the insurance and had plenty left over. But your grandmother says she has no money. Who am I to believe? Your grandmother or Mrs. Jacobs?"

"My grandmother," I said. "She's sick. She needs the powders."

"This is the last time. Tell her I'm coming over to have a talk about that bill."

When I got home from school the next day my grandmother was sewing, hunched up in the light of the little reading lamp, her face in shadow. "Mr. Finkel was here this afternoon," she said. "He tried to collect his bill. I talked him out of it but I had to humble myself to do it. Think of it, Charlie, your own grandmother on her knees in front of a Jew. Well, it's no good crying over spilt milk. We're in his power. Mr. Finkel wants you to work for him. You start Saturday morning and I don't want to hear a whimper out of you. Now finish the breakfast dishes and when you get through go down to the Boston Store and get me some material. The samples are on Mabel's bed."

I went out in the kitchen and turned on the hot water.

"Ask for Mrs. Benson. Get half a yard of each."

"I heard you," I shouted. I was mad. I didn't want to work for a Jew.

Saturday morning I showed up at Finkel's Pharmacy at eight o'clock sharp. Mr. Finkel took me in the back room and showed me where the broom was and the barrel of sweeping compound and the mop and the wooden scrub bucket and the scrub brush with the long handle. He showed me how to scrub the tile floor and how to wipe the marble baseboards around the counters with a wet rag. After that I washed the windows and polished the pumps on the soda fountain.

Mr. Finkel kept apologizing between customers. "For twenty years I have been in business. I scrub the floor, I clean, I dust. I make the sodas and roll the pills. I hire Mr. Harris to share the work. Mr. Harris is a registered pharmacist. Would he touch a broom? Mamma helps at the fountain. She keeps house upstairs. She makes out the orders, she keeps the books, she pays the bills. That I should have a boy like you, Charlie! Would I send him to work at fourteen? A boy your age should be with footballs and bats, not mops and soda fountains." When he sent me home at noon I was beginning to wonder why he hired me at all.

Saturday night they were all there when I went back, Mr. and Mrs. Finkel and Mr. Harris. Mr. Harris was a fat man with a mustache. He gave me a gray druggist's coat to wear, about two sizes too large. Mr. Finkel showed me how to make sodas and sundaes and how to mix soft drinks. He showed me how to take the empty ice cream cans down to the storage box in the basement and how to lug the new ones up and pack them in salted ice. Whenever I made a sale I gave the money to Mrs. Finkel and she cranked the sale up on the cash register and kept her eye on the change until I gave it to the customer. At ten-thirty Mr. Harris went home. At a quarter of eleven Mrs. Finkel went up the backstairs to the apartment over the store. At eleven o'clock Mr. Finkel pulled out his watch and announced it was time to close. He told me to get the wire screen out of the toilet room. I did and he fitted it over the plate glass on the front door and padlocked it into place. Then he said goodnight.

"Goodnight, my eye," I said. "When do I get paid?"

"Paid?" said Mr. Finkel. "Your grandmother owes me two-hundred-thirty dollars thirty-five cents. I call on her to collect my money. She puts me off. Mr. Finkel, she says, my grandson is looking for a job, can you use him? Mrs. Slaughter, I say, for twenty years I have been in business. I do not hire children. Mr. Finkel, she says, you understand business. Charlie is big for his age. We will make a deal."

"What deal?"

"Your grandmother says you will work out the debt." Mr. Finkel went behind the cigar counter and figured on a pad. "Thirty cents an hour. Saturday morning four hours, make it five, Saturday Monday Wednesday Friday nights, twenty hours. Every other Sunday ten. Nine dollars a week. Nine into two-hundred-thirty dollars and thirty-five cents makes twenty-five weeks and five dollars thirty-five cents over. In twenty-six weeks I will pay you in cash."

"Why you big sheeny," I shouted, slamming the door so hard it almost broke. I ran all the way home and turned on the light in my grandmother's bedroom and shook her by the shoulders.

"Wake up. I been robbed. Mr. Finkel didn't pay me."

"That's the Jews for you."

"No it isn't," I said. "It's you. You made the deal."

My grandmother sat up and reached under her pillow for her handkerchief. "It wasn't my idea," she said. "Mr. Finkel threatened to sue. I was desperate." I thought at first she was putting on an act but when I saw her crying real tears I didn't know what to think.

"I never meant to tell you this, Charlie, but when I had my gallstones out the doctor said my days were numbered. I may die tomorrow, next week, or a month from now. But I've kept alive all these years. Do you know why? Because I was thinking of you. When I go, who'll take care of you? I can't ask Mabel to support you and herself too."

"I don't want you to die."

"You mustn't think of it. Your poor mother would never forgive me if I made you go to work against your will."

"She wouldn't want us to starve."

"There, there," she said, stroking my hand. "If Mr. Finkel sends me to jail, you and Mabel will manage somehow."

"I won't let him send you to jail."

"Then kiss me goodnight and go to bed. That's better. You mustn't cry, Charlie. You're too old."

"I'm not crying," I said. "My nose is running. I must be getting a cold."

"Then use your handkerchief," said my grandmother. "That's right. Blow hard! Get all the poison out."

Monday night I went back to the drugstore and put on the jacket that was hanging in the toilet. There was a dill pickle wrapped in wax paper in the pocket.

"Mamma sent it down for you," said Mr. Finkel. "She put it in the pocket when she shortened the sleeves. It's all right. I didn't tell her what you said. Only never use that word again. All my life I listen to boys call me names. You're not like them."

I took a bite of the pickle.

"Sure. I didn't know what I was saying."

"You're a good boy, Charlie," said Mr. Finkel, "only sometimes you never seem to know it."

FOUR

In time Finkel's Pharmacy became more like a home to me than my grandmother's house on Wilton Avenue. Saturday mornings when I finished scrubbing the floor, Mrs. Finkel would invite me upstairs for a corned beef sandwich and one of her homemade dill pickles that would almost explode when you bit into it. New malted-milk mixers were put in that winter and Mr. Harris let me help myself to malteds when Mr. Finkel wasn't around. I grew quite healthy and my face became covered with pimples.

In April Mr. Finkel started paying me in cash. I took

home my first week's salary and laid it on the dining room table.

"That's fine," said my grandmother. "Get me my purse."

"It's my money."

"You can't keep it all yourself."

"Five dollars anyway."

"Two dollars a week is plenty for a boy your age," said Mabel.

"Oh for God sake," I said. "I'm not a kid any more. I'll keep at least half my pay or I'll move out."

"Then move," said my grandmother. "But don't come crawling back to me on your knees when you get sick. Don't expect me to take care of you when your mind starts to fail like your poor mother's."

I was on to Mabel and my grandmother by that time so we compromised. I would keep two dollars every week, only in addition I would ask Mr. Finkel for five cents an hour raise and keep the difference. When I asked Mr. Finkel for a raise he said he would give me forty cents an hour, a nickel more than I expected. My grandmother was dumbfounded. "That's the Jews for you!" she said. "When you least expect it is when you catch them napping most."

That summer, for the first time in my life, there was enough money in my pockets to do what I wanted. One Wednesday afternoon I took the streetcar down to the pier. The pier hadn't changed much. There was a show going on in the auditorium. I sat down in the last row and watched a flock of girls wheeling around the stage in gypsy costumes, cracking tambourines against their elbows. After the dance there was a play about early Chicago.

"What do you think of Father Marquette?" said a voice in my ear. It was Miss Ives. While I was watching she had sat down beside me. "That's Milton," she said. "He's taking your place this year. Dolly tells me you're working in a drugstore. What a shameful waste of talent."

"We need the money."

"Money's not everything, my boy. I'd love to have a talk with your grandmother one of these days. What are you doing Friday nights?"

"Working."

"You must rearrange your schedule. Mr. Oldenheimer has agreed to direct the Tuesday evening class at my studio in a series of pantomimes for the Friday evening program. All adult students of course. We'd love to have you. Here. I'll give you the address." She jotted it down in her notebook and tore out the page. When she looked up, the audience was drifting toward the doors.

"Oh dear, Milton has discovered Chicago and can't remember what comes next. Keep your seats, everybody," she sang out. "The program is not over." she wagged a finger in my direction, said "See you Tuesday," and sailed off, her long blue scarf trailing behind.

Miss Ives' studio was not what I pictured a studio would be, with tubes of paint and half-finished pictures sitting around. It consisted of three rooms and an office on the top floor of a building on Michigan Avenue with wide windows looking out over Grant Park and the lake. Miss Ives and her assistant, a small English girl by the name of Vivian Sterling, gave lessons in acting and elocution there, only they called it education in the drama. Mr. Oldenheimer gave lessons in interpretive dancing in the studio when nobody else was using it. The largest room had a small stage at one end with blue velvet curtains.

Tuesday night when I turned up, Miss Ives and Miss Sterling were sitting in the big room with about a dozen students around them, listening to one of the students give a recitation on the stage. Three of the students were schoolteachers. There were only two men. When the recitation was over, Miss Ives got up and introduced me as Mr. Flowers, a former member of the Chicago Children's Theater who had professional experience in vaudeville. The class was quite thrilled to meet a real professional, especially the schoolteachers.

Mr. Oldenheimer arrived a few minutes later in a silk shirt with big sleeves, a real bohemian if I ever saw one. He had cooked up a pantomime called the King of the Yellow Butterflies. One of the men got to be king. He had a small beer belly and spent most of his time prancing around after Miss Sterling while the rest of us walked around flapping our wings to some very modern crashing music. Mr. Oldenheimer banged on the back of the grand piano and screamed, "Remember, people, you are butterflies. Stretch your wings, people, stretch!" The pantomime only lasted ten minutes but it took two hours to rehearse. We were still rehearsing when the lights went on in Grant Park and the Navy Pier lit up like a fairyland in the distance. Rivers of sweat were running down Mr. Oldenheimer, and the ladies had to stop every now and then and wipe themselves under their arms with their handkerchiefs, especially the schoolteachers.

Mrs. Spreckels, a very scrawny and artistic lady from Hull House, was in charge of costumes down at the pier.

She passed out costumes to us Friday night, yellow night-gowns with long sleeves attached at the wrist. They looked fine in the spotlights but the pantomime was like an opera without any singing in it. The audience couldn't figure out what it was all about.

"You worked late tonight," said my grandmother when I got home.

"I wasn't working, I was down at the pier," I said without thinking. "I was a butterfly in the pantomime."

"Oh tra la la," said Mabel, waltzing around. "Charlie is a butterfly."

"Make her stop."

"I'll make you stop," said my grandmother. "A big boy like you a butterfly! I never heard of such a thing."

The next pantomime was the Virgin of the Nile. Miss Sterling was the virgin and we had to sacrifice her to the crocodiles in the River Nile. After that came the French Revolution. In that one we wore rags and beat on dishpans. The next week it was Bluebeard and His Seven Wives. The other two men had quit by that time so I got to be Blue-beard. Mrs. Spreckels made a long beard of rope and dyed it blue. Everyone wore Turkish costumes with long transparent pants. When I got home that night, my grandmother said, "Well, what were you doing tonight?"

"I worked late," I said.

"Don't lie, Charlie. I went down to the pier with Mabel to see for myself. I know where you were. Who were all those naked women?"

"They were schoolteachers."

"Amanda, I don't think you should allow him to go down to that place. Women that run around the stage naked like that are a danger to society. Do they ever make any advances to you, Charlie?"

"None of your business," I said. "I bring money into this house. I got a right to do what I want."

"Did you hear what he said, Mabel? You can see what that bunch of bohemians are doing to my grandson."

"Let me handle this," said Mabel. "You're not old enough to realize what those women are after, Charlie. Just because they have the money and the time they think they can ruin a clean young boy like you and get away with it. Have any of them ever tried to handle your privates?"

"Mabel!"

"We might as well be frank, Amanda. If he gets some terrible disease and goes blind, we'd only have ourselves to blame."

"You leave me alone," I shouted, running into the bathroom and locking the door. "I know what I'm doing."

"You're making a fool of yourself, that's what you're doing," screamed my grandmother through the door. "If you go down to that pier any more you'll wind up in Dunning like your poor mother."

My grandmother was right. I had been making a fool of myself but I was too blinded by the spotlights to notice. Monday night Dolly came into Finkel's Pharmacy for a vanilla soda. "You should have been down at the pier this afternoon," she said. "You should have heard what happened. The mothers' club had a special meeting about last Friday's pantomime. They said the women didn't have anything on under their pants and neither did the men."

"That's a lie."

"Well, the stage was too dark, I couldn't tell. Anyway

there aren't going to be any more pantomimes. They're giving the pier an immoral name."

"Vanilla sodas are ten cents," I said. "Just in case you forgot."

"Don't worry, I'll pay for it," said Dolly, reaching into her slipper bag for her purse. "Oh, I almost forgot to congratulate you. I was certainly glad to hear you passed seventh grade last June. It was about time."

Poor Dolly, she had grown up quite plain. She started high school that year. So did Stinko but Stinko wouldn't have anything to do with her, because Dolly still wore her hair in long curls like twisted brass. It was harder for me to get away from her. She was always dropping into the drugstore for vanilla sodas. One night in September she sat down at the soda fountain and said, "Charlie, were your ears burning this afternoon? Because Miss Ives was talking about you. She wants you to join the Friday afternoon class at her studio. It needs boys."

"Don't get me mixed up with that kid stuff," I said. "Now get out of here before I squirt soda water all over your slipper bag." But I went downtown Friday after school just to find out what Dolly was talking about. There were two boys in that class, Milton from the pier, and a halfwit with adenoids whose mother dragged him in from Lake Forest every week on the North Shore electric. Dolly and the other kids did recitations and rehearsed a play.

"What do you think of our little class?" Miss Ives said to me afterwards. "Would you like to join?"

"I can't afford it."

"My dear boy, you are here as my guest. I'm not interested in your money. I'm interested in your future."

"But I don't want to be an actor. I want to be a dancer."

"Splendid. Join the Friday class and I'll see that Mr. Oldenheimer gives you all the lessons you want."

"I don't mean that kind of dancing. I mean softshoe," I said, thinking that would stop her, "I mean tap."

"Sometimes I wish your viewpoint weren't quite so professional. Let me think. Have you ever heard of Mr. Barney? He's an old Ziegfeld man. Your father probably knew him. I've sent dozens of pupils to him. It's time he did me a favor in return. I'll see what I can arrange."

Mr. Barney turned out to be an old man, about five-feet-four. His dancing days were over but he had plenty of fresh routines and many professionals came to him for workouts and ideas. He had a studio with a beat-up piano in it and a cracked mirror in a building on Randolph Street full of theatrical booking agencies. The first time I went there he rattled off a complicated routine but I couldn't follow him any more than I could follow a grasshopper. He told me to come back when I got some decent taps put on my shoes. He wasn't used to handling charity cases.

When I went back a week later he seemed surprised I showed up at all. He said the reason he acted so peculiar the week before was the way Miss Ives spoke to him on the phone. She talked like he owed her the world. "Miss Ives said you were a Ziegfeld man," I said. Mr. Barney laughed. "That woman doesn't know me from Adam but she's heard of Ziegfeld," he said. "She's name-crazy."

I took to Mr. Barney the way a duck takes to water and he took to me the same way. The more I learned the more he piled it on. Every afternoon when I wasn't working

I practiced in the basement until my lungs clogged up with coal dust and the lady on the first floor complained to my grandmother. On an average of once a week I would cut eighth grade and go downtown to McVickers or the Oriental Theater where the big bands played and sit through two shows and try to memorize the routines of the dancers I saw there. Whenever I got impatient Mr. Barney would shake his head. I was young yet. When the time came he would see that I got the right kind of break. In the meantime it was a pleasure to teach someone who had their brains in their feet. I was to take that as a compliment he said. When he found out I was working, he said it was only fair I should pay him a little on account to keep it from looking like charity, so I did.

Lucy Ives never asked for money. All she wanted was to use me as bait for her Friday afternoon class and she got what she wanted. We put on all sorts of stuff in that class that would pass for plays. I was a quack doctor in one about a little girl that wouldn't take her castor oil and we gave it at doctor's conventions and in hotel ballrooms until I thought I would go crazy. We even went on the radio. Once a month we would gather round a microphone in the Hotel La Salle. A couple of fat men posing as uncles would sing a lullaby while children all over Chicago crawled into bed with their earphones on. Then we would recite a play about Jack Frost or King Winter. My specialty was making a long low noise like the wind.

In the wintertime Miss Ives wore dresses that buttoned high around her throat, thin dark-colored scarves, and always a hat, indoors and out. She was like her clothes, not up-to-date but never out-of-date either. Opera singers in mink coats were always bumping into her in elevators and kissing her on the cheek and calling her dear. But there was something lonesome about her in spite of the fact that she knew everybody and everybody knew her, not in the way an ordinary person is lonesome but almost like you might say I was lonesome in school among all those kids whose voices hadn't even changed yet. My future got to be sort of a burning ambition with her. Dancing was all very well she said, but my education came first. I kidded her along.

"Where am I going to get the money to go to college?"

"You think entirely too much about money, my boy. There are scholarships to be had. If not, perhaps I can find you a benefactor."

Lucy Ives was a big subject of conversation around our house. Mabel had a theory Miss Ives was trying to turn me into a chorus boy. My grandmother thought the dancing I did in the basement was connected with the pier somehow. "But it's winter," I explained. "The pier is closed." Then where did I spend all my spare time she wanted to know.

"At Miss Ives' studio."

"Why Charlie," said Mabel, "you never told us she had a studio. Just last Sunday I was reading about one of those studio parties in the paper. Amanda, you have no idea what goes on at those places."

"I read the papers too, Mabel. One of these days I'm going down to that place and find out for myself."

Things went along like that until one Friday afternoon in March when I was sitting next to Milton in Miss Ives' studio, listening to Dolly recite a scene from a play. Suddenly the curtains in the little doorway beside the stage parted and my grandmother walked in. Miss Ives stood up, holding her notebook in front of her like a shield.

"That's my grandmother," I said.

"Why Mrs. Flowers, how nice."

"Slaughter," said my grandmother.

"I beg your pardon. Mrs. Slaughter. I've been wanting to meet you for ever so long. Won't you sit down? Visitors are always welcome. Go on, Dolly dear. Dolly has been giving us a reading from *The Doll's House.* I thought Ibsen was beyond high school sophomores but Dolly doesn't seem to think so. You know *The Doll's House* of course."

My grandmother gave the blue velvet curtains on the stage a poke like she expected a couple of naked women to come tumbling out. When nothing happened she said, "Why yes," and sat down. After the class she had a long talk with Miss Ives. When they came out of the office they were both covered with smiles.

"You never told me what an interesting grandmother you had, Charles. I've been trying to convince her she should attend one of our adult classes."

"Oh my! I don't think Charlie would approve of that."

"Well now that you've found us, come down more often. Any time at all. We're like Tennyson's brook. Men may come and men may go but we go on forever."

My grandmother kept her mouth shut until we got on the elevated. Then she plunked herself down and said, "What was that about the brook? Who is this man Tennyson?"

"Search me. Miss Ives is always talking about him."

"Well, if Miss Ives knows him, he must be almost as famous as John Barrymore. You know, Charlie, it pays to find out things for yourself. Mabel's been giving me the wrong impression of that woman right along. If I were you, I'd follow Miss Ives' advice. Give up this dancing nonsense. Become an actor and you'll be worth a pile of money someday. It's actors they want now, what with talking pictures and the radio and all. The trouble with you is you don't know a good thing when you see it. Miss Ives can do a lot for you. Why, the way she talked I wouldn't be surprised if she'd send you to college someday."

"Oh for God sake, you can't go to college unless you go to high school first."

"I wouldn't be too sure about that. Miss Ives might be able to fix it. You be nice to her now."

The following Friday when I came home from school, my grandmother was all dressed up. She had some of Mabel's lipstick on and some of her rouge and she looked awful. "Change your shirt," she said. "We don't want to keep Miss Ives waiting. We're late as it is."

"I'm not going anywhere," I said. "And neither are you. You're letting Miss Ives make a fool out of you just like she did out of me."

"Don't talk to me like that. I won't have it. If you won't think of your future, I'll have to think of it for you. Now hurry up and change your shirt."

When I refused, she started to cry. When that didn't do any good, she offered to throw me out of the house. "I don't care what you do," I said. "I'm not going down to that place again. I've got my own life to live."

"Well, live it then. Live it out in Finkel's Pharmacy for all I care, but don't come to me ten years from now and ask me why I didn't help you plan your future when you were still young."

"Don't worry," I said. "I won't."

Everything was changing in that neighborhood. The Melody Gardens weren't the showplace they used to be. They changed hands the year before and opened with a big fanfare on Decoration Day but went broke before summer was over. The next year they didn't even bother to open. Everything was changing—the neighborhood, the Melody Gardens, even Finkel's Pharmacy. For a long time business had been falling off so Mr. Finkel decided to move. He sank all of his savings in a new store in Wildwood on the Northwest Side. It was too far for me to travel after school so I lost my job.

I didn't care. I became sixteen that year and quit school forever. When I looked around for a man-sized job it turned out nobody wanted to hire a boy who never went to high school. "Suit yourself," said my grandmother, "but if I were you I'd call up Mr. Finkel and see if he could use a full-time boy." By that time I decided never to do anything my grandmother said. I wasn't a boy any more, and Mr. Barney had agreed to give me lessons on credit until I found another job. But bad news came in bunches that year, like bananas. That was a year of change for Mr. Barney too. When I went downtown two weeks later, his door was locked. I asked the elevator starter where I could get in touch with him.

"Brazil," he said. "He got a job with a coffee company."

I went right on practicing for a while but whatever it

was Mr. Barney put into my feet he took to Brazil with him. I practiced less and less and finally quit altogether. They weren't the same feet without Mr. Barney around. Well, I still had my dreams, my poor dreams. In the meantime I hung on, waiting for a job to turn up or for something to happen. Nothing happened until August. That was when the telegram came.

The telegram was from Lucy Ives. Who else ever sent a telegram to our house? It said to get in touch with her about a job so at noon the next day I walked into the building on Michigan Avenue. Miss Sterling was in the office, pecking at a typewriter with one finger. When I asked her what it was all about, she said, "I wouldn't know. Lucy's been ill. She loves to send telegrams but she seldom remembers what she's said in them. Perhaps it has to do with the pageant. It's Merrie England this year. Milton was to have been court jester but he has the mumps. You can wait in the studio if you wish."

I went in the big room. Through the wide windows I could see Lake Michigan, gray and covered with whitecaps under the clouds. The Navy Pier looked small and far away. Suddenly the rain began to slam against the window ledge, blotting out the pier in a gray drizzle. When Miss Ives came in a few minutes later, her white dress was covered with rain splotches. She had on an old felt hat with a piece of fur sticking out the side of it like a rabbit's foot, and a rose-colored scarf. She looked different somehow.

"It's good to see you again," she said, shaking my hand. "Did Miss Sterling tell you the news? Milton has the mumps and we need a new jester. There's not much time. I'll give you a rough idea of the pageant." She laid her notebook on the grand piano and leafed through the pages while the rain drummed against the windows and played a solo on the sill. "Here we are. All aboard for Merrie England. Scene one. Sporting on the village green. Two. Mummers in the innyard. Scene three. Hawkers in the streets of London. Four. Maypole number. Five. Joyous dance. The mothers are performers this year. Six. Will Shakespeare and Bottom in his ass's head. Seven. Tournament. Eight. Grand finale. That should give you a rough idea. We'll go through the details later. Charles! I don't think you've listened to a word I've said."

"I was watching the rain."

"Horrible weather, isn't it? Let's hope it clears in time for Ravinia tomorrow. Have you any questions?"

"Yes," I said. "What about that job?"

"What job?"

"The one in the telegram."

One end of the rose-colored scarf slipped off Lucy Ives' shoulder. It wasn't until she tossed it back over her shoulder that I noticed she'd been using her left hand all along, while her right hand hung limp like a dead flipper under the scarf. Maybe that was what Miss Sterling meant by her being ill. She saw me looking at her hand and said, "Dolly did tell me you were unemployed, now that I think of it. But if all you care about is jobs and money, I'm not at all sure I want to have you in the pageant."

"You can't blame me for asking."

"Don't be so mercenary, Charles. If you value your time so highly I'll make it up to you. Now let's not be rude to each other again. We'll have a bite to eat. Then we'll take a taxi to the pier."

There was a rehearsal at one o'clock in the auditorium on the pier but the rain rumbled so hard on the skylight Miss Ives couldn't make herself heard. When I climbed the stairs to the costume room an hour later, the rain was still lashing against the red brick walls of the tower, the waves were still thumping against the sides of the pier. In the costume room, a can of radiator paint had fallen off a table and covered the floor with silver powder. Mrs. Spreckels ran in and pulled a donkey's head off a shelf. "Damnation! I almost forgot Bottom. Oh yes, you want the jester's costume. Here!" She tossed me a bundle of rags and dashed out the door with the donkey's head under her arm. I went downstairs and unrolled the bundle in the dressing room, where about fifty boys were squirting mouthfuls of water at each other. All at once they shut up like clams. Miss Ives was standing in the doorway.

"Charles! You're not dressed. We're ready to begin."

"The tights don't fit."

She glared at me a minute, then she went down like a balloon with all the air going out of it. "Just watch then. It really doesn't matter. There's only a handful of spectators. Have Mrs. Spreckels give you another pair of tights for tomorrow."

Lucy Ives was right. It didn't matter. The pageant was terrible. One of the mothers laced her corset too tight and fell in a faint when she bowed to Queen Elizabeth. Half the audience stood up to see what happened. The other half walked out. They thought it was over I guess. That night every elevated in Chicago went banging by our kitchen window. I had nightmares all night long—of myself running up and down the elevated tracks in a pair of red tights and a cap with bells on it while people threw vegetables at me out of their kitchen windows.

Thursday was warm and full of sunshine. There was the same grandstand at Ravinia, the same green trees in the background, the same silver water tower among the trees. I leaned against the grandstand, soaking up the morning sunshine, and watched Miss Ives direct the dress rehearsal through a megaphone. "Positions! Last figure of the dance. Don't walk. Stride! Mrs. O'Brien, if you're going to faint again, go home."

Suddenly the rehearsal stopped. Lucy Ives stared at me for a few seconds, then she came charging across the field in my direction like an elephant with its ears extended. When she was three feet away she stopped.

"Throw that cigarette away. You're a performer, Charles, not a spectator. Get out on that field. Do something."

"Do what?"

"Romp. Dance. Act the clown. You're very good at that."

So I romped and danced and acted the clown while the sweat poured down my forehead and the bells jingled on my cap. I was very good at it.

The grandstand was full by two-fifteen. At two-thirty the bandleader lifted his baton and the band burst into the overture. When the overture was over, Miss Ives raised her megaphone. That was the signal. I ran out and turned a somersault and motioned the townspeople on. An hour later they were still coming, townspeople, jugglers, kings, queens, knights, hawkers, ladies, dancers, pages. The colored streamers wound round and round the maypoles and then unwound and wound again in time to the music. The knights knocked each other on the head with wooden sticks and rolled in the grass on their chicken-wire horses. The silver water tower rose among the trees behind them like the tower of a castle.

Lucy Ives stood next to the bandmaster the whole time, her notebook open on a sort of pulpit in front of her, turning the pages with her left hand. When the first wave of applause rippled over the grandstand, a smile spread over her broad flat face. She turned and made a bow to the bandmaster and then they both made a bow to the audience and the long blue scarf fluttered out behind her in the breeze like it was taking a little bow of its own.

Ravinia was in a class by itself in those days. The open-air opera house was surrounded by gravel paths and flowerbeds and geraniums. You could watch the opera free if you sat on the benches outside the pavilion. I had never seen an opera before so I stayed to watch it that night. During the intermission Miss Ives wanted to go for a walk so we walked through the crowds and among the flowerbeds until we came to the pageant field. The empty grandstand was in shadow but the moon lit up the silver water tower and the grass. Miss Ives was still talking about the pageant.

"You were splendid, Charles. You have great talents, great gifts."

"I can't do anything except dance a little."

"Don't underestimate yourself, my boy. I'd like to repay you for what you did this afternoon."

"What about that job?" I said.

"Oh yes! Thank you for reminding me. It was just an idea but it's worth exploring. You've been taking lessons from that Barney person for almost a year now. How would you like to teach simple tap routines to the older boys at the pier next summer? There's no hurry. Think it over and let me know after the first of the year. Isn't that the orchestra? We'd better go back to the pavilion."

We started back. I was too surprised to say anything. In the first place Mr. Barney was in Brazil. In the second place I needed a job now, not next summer. While I was still trying to think of something to say, Miss Ives said, "I'm sorry about the way I spoke to you this morning, but you should have known better than to smoke in front of the children. You're just a boy."

"I'm sixteen."

"Then you'll graduate soon."

"I already did."

"Congratulations, Charles. I had no idea you'd graduated. Have you decided on a college yet?"

"How can I go to college when I never went to high school?"

"But my dear boy, you just said you'd graduated."

"From eighth grade," I said. "Then I quit school. Now I'm looking for a job."

Lucy Ives stopped in the middle of the path. A little breeze came up and fluttered her scarf. For once she didn't bother to fuss with it.

"You're joking of course."

"Why should I joke about it?"

"You make a fine jester but you can't play the fool

forever. If what you say is true, you've hurt me, Charles. But you've hurt yourself more. Tell me, my boy, what is it you want out of life?"

"I don't want anything," I said.

We stood there for a minute, listening to the music that was all mixed up with the smell of flowers in the flowerbeds.

"That's the 'Barcarolle,' " said Miss Ives. "Lovely, isn't it? Bori sings it. Would you like to meet her, Charles?"

"I don't like opera," I said. "I think I'll go home."

"Do as you wish. You would anyway," she said, holding out her left hand for me to shake. "Thank you again for all you've done. Goodnight, my dear."

My dear! Nobody ever called me that before. But I didn't fall for it. I was on to Miss Ives by that time, just like I was on to Mabel and my grandmother. I didn't want to have anything more to do with any of them.

I was changing too.

FIVE

One day long ago, when I was still in fourth grade, the teacher explained how a bunch of men got the Chicago River to flow backward instead of forward by connecting it to a canal that flowed into another river that flowed into the Mississippi. That way they were able to flush all the garbage and dead dogs into the Mississippi instead of Lake Michigan. It seemed like a good idea at the time, said the teacher, but if the river flowed backwards long enough it would suck all the water out of Lake Michigan. That seemed like a sound idea too, but like lots of ideas in this world it didn't hold water, or else it held too much because the level of Lake Michigan rose several feet that winter until there was more water in it than the little Chicago River could drain away in a hundred years. That was a wild winter. The mist rolled in off the lake. The foghorns grunted day and night. When the wind was high, the waves washed over Lake Shore Drive and smashed windows on the Navy Pier.

While the wind snarled around the Loop and boats went down all over, another storm began to blow. It lasted longer than the storms of that winter and nobody was able to do much about it, any more than they were able to stop the waves from smashing against the Navy Pier. They called it the depression. It's all there in the old newspapers if you have any left in your basement.

The depression began with a stock market crash. I was never sure what a stock market was or how it could crash but it did and right after it crashed my grandmother became interested in it. In later years Mabel used to pride herself on how she made my grandmother sell before she got completely wiped out. Maybe she did but when it came to acting poor nobody could hold a candle to my grandmother and when the stock market continued to go down she acted as if the whole Chicago River backed up in her face. Mabel was still working as collection agent for the jewelry firm. She had her own ideas as to what my grandmother should do with the money that was left. One night she brought a diamond ring home on approval and stuck it under my grandmother's nose as she sat poring over the falling stock market reports at the dining room table. According to Mabel, diamonds were the safest investment you could make, safer even than playing the horses. My grandmother turned the ring from side to side in the light of the little reading lamp. She shook her head and handed it back.

"You can't eat diamonds, Mabel. With Charlie out of work, I wouldn't be able to pay for it anyway."

That was the darkest year of the depression. Everyone that had a job was holding onto it for dear life. Mabel and my grandmother wanted me to apply for a job at Mr. Finkel's new drugstore in Wildwood but I was too proud to go crawling back to Mr. Finkel and spent my days downtown instead, filling out applications for jobs in department stores and wholesale houses and banks. One night when I had been out of work for almost a year my grandmother looked up from the evening paper and said, "Miss Ives is dead. Did you hear that, Mabel? Miss Ives died yesterday. Charlie never even told me she was sick."

"I think that's terrible, Amanda. He never tells you anything. Who gets all her money?"

"I don't know but she must have left a lot. She was going to send Charlie through college once."

"She was always talking," I said. "It didn't mean anything."

"Maybe not, but you're going to the funeral Wednesday and find out. You find out who her lawyer is and when the will is being read. If you're ashamed to do it, I'll go myself."

"I'll go," I said. "I got nothing else to do." So Wednesday morning I took the Jackson Park elevated to the funeral parlor on the South Side. The mothers from the pier were out in force. Mrs. O'Brien had fainted as usual and Mrs. Hennessy was waving a bottle of smelling salts under her nose. Benny Hirschfield's mother was spreading the rumor Miss Ives died because she had a goiter, that was why she always wore a scarf. When it came time to file by the rubber-tired coffin carriage I took a good look but I couldn't tell. There was a white scarf around her neck but it was full of starch and looked as dead as the hair.

When I went outside, Miss Sterling was standing on the sidewalk, trying hard not to cry. "I'm so glad you could come," she said, squeezing my hand. "Lucy was always so fond of you, Charles."

"What about the will?"

"What will?" she said, dropping my hand. "If it's money you're after, you've come to the wrong place. Lucy left her affairs in a terrible state."

"I'm out of work," I explained. "I just wondered if you knew of a job."

"If I knew of a good job, I'd take it myself," she said and walked away without saying good-bye. I stood there on the sidewalk trying to squeeze out a few tears for old times' sake, but I wasn't much good at a funeral I guess. I couldn't cry any more than I could pray.

After the funeral I went back to jobhunting. Every morning my grandmother doled me out carfare and pocket money and every morning I took the elevated downtown and went from department store to department store and from bank to bank to see what happened to the applications I filled out the autumn before. Spring came. The cotton-woods blossomed. One gray May day I decided to swallow my pride and take the streetcar to Wildwood and ask Mr. Finkel for my old job back.

It was a four-block walk from the streetcar, a long cold

walk past a sprinkling of quiet bungalows and over a little footbridge that crossed the north branch of the Chicago River before it joined the drainage canal. During the twenties Wildwood had been a real pioneering neighborhood. The woods had been cut down, the streets had been laid out and here and there an apartment building had been built. But the depression took the wind out of the boom and now the empty sidewalks and the fireplugs stretched for blocks into the country.

The Wildwood Pharmacy was in one of the new apartment buildings with an elm tree growing out of a hole in the sidewalk. It had a brand-new soda fountain with automatic refrigeration. Everything was modern and up-to-date. I must have looked hungry because the first thing Mr. Finkel did was lift the lid of the hot fudge machine and fix me a hot fudge sundae. While I ate the sundae we talked about my grandmother and about the old drugstore near the Melody Gardens.

"I won't lie to you," said Mr. Finkel. "I would like to have you back. So would Mamma. But business is bad. We run the store ourselves except when the hot weather starts. You know what I pay the high school boys now? Thirty cents an hour."

"I'll take twenty."

"Believe me, Charlie, it's for your own good. This is no job for a young man starting out in life."

I reached in my pocket and pulled out two dimes and slammed them on the counter. Mr. Finkel looked at them through his thick glasses. Then he looked at me. "What's that for?"

"For the sundae, you big sheeny."

Mr. Finkel shook his head. "Why don't you grow up?" he said. "You don't say that word like you meant it any more. That's the only difference."

I walked out, leaving the two dimes on the counter. There was only three cents left in my pocket so I had to walk home. It was six miles. It sprinkled a little, then it poured. I ticked off the blocks, eight to a mile. I learned that in fourth grade too. When I got home I was soaked to the skin. My face was burning.

"Where have you been all this time?" snapped my grandmother. "Did you get the job?"

I lay down on the cot in the kitchen and refused to open my mouth to answer her or even to eat. The next morning she called a doctor.

"You'd better get some food into that boy," said the doctor. "He's undernourished."

The doctor was right but I didn't want to live any more. When anyone came near me with food I turned my face to the wall and thought of all the people I had ever liked—my father, Minnie, Stinko, Miss Ives, Miss Sterling, Mr. Barney. It was like they were all dead and I wanted to be dead too. But after three days I got hungry and accepted a bowl of tomato soup and decided to live. It was a good thing I changed my mind because that very night Mabel came home with good news. She had a new boyfriend, a Mr. Nelson who worked in Finley and Dunlap's department store downtown. He was very influential with the owners and could offer me a job as a stockboy for twelve-fifty a week starting Monday.

So the depression was over as far as we were concerned. Looking back on it now, I think maybe everything would have turned out different if it hadn't been for the depression. But then anything might turn out different, only it never does.

SIX

Finley and Dunlap's was an old-fashioned department store on the west side of State Street. Everything about it was old-fashioned from the elevators that went clanking up the forty-year-old elevator shafts to the chandeliers, which were former gas globes with electric lights installed inside them. Halfway between State and Dearborn Streets was the most old-fashioned thing of all, a circular stairway that had been the wonder of the store when it opened in 1890. At the bottom of the stairwell was a marble fountain ringed with notion counters and filled with ferns, a beautiful target for suicide jumpers. On each landing was a circular showcase filled with merchandise—silver on the second, ladies' hats on the third, and so on all the way up to the eighth floor where you could buy the most expensive fire pokers and washing machines in Chicago. The top of the stairwell was covered with a dome of colored glass showing three nymphs pouring a mixture of water and stars out of vases they carried upside down on their shoulders. A skylight on the ninth floor made the colored glass dome glow like a church window, but if you were an employee called up to the ninth floor to get bawled out or fired, you could see the other side of the dome like a sock turned inside out, oozing plaster and stained-glass cement.

In spite of the salaries, which were kept at an 1890 level like everything else, Finley and Dunlap's was considered the type of place refined people would give their right arm to work at. Nobody shopped at Finley's to save money. You knew in advance you were going to have to pay for being waited on by a saleslady with creamy white hair and a pair of glasses on a chain that rolled up inside a gold button on the bosom, who had been there almost as long as the floorwalker with the toupee.

Mr. Nelson, the supervisor of stockboys, had been at Finley's for twenty years. Six months after I started working, he and Mabel broke up because of Mrs. Nelson. After that he began looking for an excuse to get rid of me but I was one of his best stockboys by then. Working as a stockboy meant shining your shoes more often and wearing a linen jacket as you pushed the merchandise trucks from one floor to another but I won't say I didn't like it. It was like being turned loose in a rich lady's bedroom. I can still close my eyes and smell the soap counter on the main floor next to the fountain and see the gleaming mirrors in their gilt frames that loomed up everywhere on the seventh floor among the misses' dresses and the stylish stouts.

Most of the salesladies were afraid to joke with the stockboys in front of the floorwalkers for fear their names would be turned in to the ninth floor, but there was another class of salesladies that worked for the hell of it, debutantes from the North Shore whose mothers and grandmothers had shopped at Finley's all their lives and who were having a fling at earning their own cigarette money before getting married. It was easy to tell the rich girls by the clothes they wore and the snotty way they treated the customers. I never spoke to them if I could help it but one day I took a load of housecoats up to the seventh floor and the only salesgirl in sight was a young blond. Salesladies had to wear black. This one's dress was black all right but it was expensive-looking and she wore her hair in a tight blond bun at the back of her neck. She was busy insulting a customer so I took the dust protector off the housecoats and leaned against a counter and watched an old lady in a maid's uniform wiping the mouthpiece of the telephone on the buyer's desk as if someone just spit on it with a mouthful of arsenic. Pretty soon the blond came over.

"These look as if you ran them off on an old Singer," she said and began tossing the housecoats onto the counter as if they were so many rags. One slipped on the floor. I picked it up and said, "Watch what you're doing. I'm not your houseboy."

The blond raised one eyebrow.

"You know what I mean. I can spot you society dames a mile off."

"Evidently you've never taken psychology or you wouldn't make such snap judgments," said the blond. "Tell me, what would you say Listerine Annie over there puts on the tissues she uses to wipe the telephones?"

"Listerine. It says so on the bottle."

"Actually, darling, the bottle contains a cheap antiseptic made by the gallon in cosmetics on the fifth floor. But a bottle with a Listerine label makes a better impression on the customers. So appearances can be deceiving. What on earth are you blushing at?"

"Watch who you're calling darling," I said.

"You love it," said the blond.

That was as close as I came to breaking into high society at Finley and Dunlap's.

Now that I was working steady, Mabel went to work on my grandmother again about the diamonds. Just think, she said, if my grandmother put all her money into diamonds she could pay the balance on monthly installments out of my salary and the diamonds would never be affected by falling stock markets and muddy tracks. My grandmother gave in and bought two diamond rings. She bought them on time so Mabel would get a commission on the monthly collections. She never wore the rings. She kept them in a flannel pouch. Once a day she would pull down all the shades, take them out of the pouch, and lay them on the dining room table and look at them in the bright overhead light. Mabel had the reading lamp in her own room now.

My best friend at Finley's was a stockboy named Richard who was always talking about the low pay and what a bastard Mr. Nelson was. He took the Wilson Avenue Local like I did so we always rode home together. One night that summer I was waiting for him at the State Street door when I saw the blond from the dress section coming down the aisle. Last minute shoppers turned to stare, then looked away embarrassed. There was a big lily sticking out of her hair. She spotted me just as Richard came up from the basement. "Hello darling," she said, taking my arm. "May I buy you a drink?"

Richard's eyeballs almost dropped out. Suddenly I got the feeling that if anything was ever going to happen to me it was now or never, so I said "See you tomorrow" to Richard and walked out with the blond on my arm. At the corner of Washington and State we had to wait for the lights. Everyone was looking at the blond instead of the lights. "Excuse me," I said. "There's a flower sticking out of your hair."

"Yes I know. I put it there."

"I suppose you could also take it out."

"Not now. We're being followed. That's Mr. Albertson behind us. He's the floorwalker on the seventh floor. The buyer in lingerie had some calla lilies on her desk and Mr. Albertson bet me ten dollars I wouldn't stick a lily in my hair and pick up the first man I met and buy him a drink. The ten dollars began as a loan. I cooked up the bet so I wouldn't have to pay it back. Albertson added the business about the pickup. He didn't think I'd dare."

"Where are we going to get a drink?" I said. It was still being prohibition in this country.

"In the poolroom over the Blackhawk."

I didn't think any girl would have nerve enough to walk into a poolroom with a lily sticking out the top of her head but the blond did. A dozen men were playing pool in their shirtsleeves in the twilight cast by Marshall Field's across the street. Next to the tables was a long lunch counter. We sat down on a couple of high stools and the blond took the flower out of her hair and laid it on the counter.

"Good evening, Miss Werner," said the gray-haired black man behind the bar.

"Two beers, George. Easy on the yeast."

It was real bootleg beer. There was a layer of yeast in the bottom of each bottle when George got through pouring. "This will knock your teeth out," said the blond. "May I have a cigarette to cushion the blow?"

I gave her one and said, "I had you figured wrong. I spotted you right off for one of those North Shore society girls."

"Indeed?" she said, looking pleased. "Why?"

"The way you act. And that dress you wear."

"You're very observant. This is the last decent rag I bought before Daddy died. It comes from Belke-Wiel's. By the way, my name is Margaret Werner. Will you have dinner with me? I'll pay for it."

"Why should you pay for it?"

"Don't be conventional or you'll bore me. You can buy me a dinner sometime when I'm broke. I'm always broke."

"I'll have to call my grandmother first."

"I've heard of men being tied to their mother's apron

strings. This is the first time I've heard of one being tied to his grandmother's."

"You win," I said. "Where do we eat?"

"Chloe's. That's a cheap restaurant on 47th Street."

"It sounds like a swamp."

"It is," said the blond.

It only took ten minutes to get to 47th Street on the Illinois Central electric. We walked up a sidewalk bordered with grocery and dry goods stores until we came to a little restaurant. Its walls were covered with murals of green trees hung with black moss against a red sky.

"No wonder they call it Chloe's," I said.

"But nobody calls it that except myself, darling. I have my own name for everything."

While we were eating, Miss Werner wanted to know how long I had worked at Finley's. I said a year. "Too long," she said. "I wouldn't be there myself if Daddy hadn't died. Daddy was a good egg but he taught me to spend money like a drunken sailor. That was how I got the job. They're still taking five dollars a week out of my pay to settle my account." She shoved the breadpudding aside when it came and lit a cigarette. "I don't intend to work at Finley's forever," she went on. "I'd like to design clothes, not sell them. Women's clothes could be so wonderful but the unfortunate truth is that ninety-nine percent of them are atrocious. Will you call the waitress, darling?" When the waitress came, Miss Werner complained there were ashes in her coffee.

"I didn't put them there," said the waitress.

"I don't care who put them there. Bring me another cup."

When the coffee came, she dipped the tip of her cigarette in the coffee. Then she laid the butt in the saucer and said, "Ready, darling?"

"Where do we go now?"

"Down to the lake to sit on some rocks. But first I'm going home to change my clothes."

Margaret Werner lived on a street called Oakenwald in a row house whose rear end faced the IC tracks. She told me to wait, she would be down in five minutes. It was closer to thirty but I didn't mind. I sat on the curb and watched the kids jumping rope in the street. The street lights came on and the kids kept right on jumping. When Miss Werner came out she was wearing slacks and her hair was hanging loose down her back, the color of molasses taffy. "Sorry to keep you waiting," she said, "but my land-lady is the ancient redhead who works in the information booth at Finley's and I had to listen to the day's scandal. Mrs. O'Reilly doesn't miss a trick."

During the 1920s the land between the IC tracks and the lake had been filled in. Now it was partly sodded and planted with new trees and bushes. Just beyond the Outer Drive was the old breakwater, two rows of pilings filled with chunks of upended rock, piled every which way. We picked out a high rock and sat down. The land came to a point there and you could see for miles up and down the shore. To the south you could see the red fire of the steel mills against the sky. To the north you could see the high buildings of the Loop. It was a hot night and all up and down the rocks, people were fishing in the dark or swimming or just cooling off. Not far away a whole family was passing the black shadow of a baby buggy onto the rocks, hand over hand, against the lights of the Outer Drive.

"This is sure a busy place," I said.

"Two years ago it was practically deserted," said Miss Werner. "The night I moved into Mrs. O'Reilly's I went swimming naked from this very rock."

"Alone?"

"But of course. Give me a cigarette, please."

There was a splash down the rocks, then some gurgles and a laugh. Two people were kissing each other in the shadow of the pilings.

"This would be a good place for smooching," I suggested.

Miss Werner smiled and tapped the cigarette on her thumbnail while I held the light.

"Tell me, what kind of a girl do you think I am? I've studied psychology as you've probably gathered by now, so you might as well be frank."

"Well, there are things about you that floor a guy," I said. "Like the way you talked to that waitress in Chloe's. Having a college education doesn't make you better than her."

"You're very observant, but only up to a point. I don't have any patience with stupidity, whether I find it in customers or in waitresses."

"Then you won't have much patience with me. I'm plenty stupid myself."

"On the contrary, you're refreshing. If you weren't, I wouldn't be wasting my time on you. And I don't have a college education, only half a one. I had to leave school when Daddy died. Aside from my bad manners, what else don't you like about me?"

"The way you wear your hair at work. The first time I saw you I wanted to call you Maggie because of that bun in back. It made me think of Maggie and Jiggs in the funny papers."

"That bun, as you call it, is extremely smart right now. Incidentally, Daddy was the only one who ever called me Maggie and got away with it. I think Daddy would have liked you, by the way. Isn't there anything about me you like?"

"You have nice legs."

"That's definitely not true. They're too long. At the University of Chicago they used to say I had the longest legs on the campus."

"If you didn't wear those high heels they wouldn't seem so long."

"Do you really think so?" she said as if I had just made a great discovery. I moved my leg closer to hers. She crossed her legs. I took hold of her hand. "Look darling," she said, freeing her hand to point. "I don't mean to change the subject, but do you see the lights on top of that boat. They move up and down like a seesaw. Why do you suppose they do that?"

"That's the rocker arm on the *Florida*," I explained. "The *Florida's* a side-wheeler that goes back and forth between Jackson Park and the Navy Pier in the summertime. The rocker arm has lights on it. When the paddle-wheels turn, it rocks up and down."

"How clever of you to know. Those lights have fascinated me for weeks. Most things do that I can't figure out. How long have you lived in this godforsaken town?"

"Eighteen years. All my life. How old are you?"

"Twenty-one, damn it," she said, flipping her cigarette in the water. "You make me feel like a cradle-snatcher. What did you do before you worked at Finley's?"

"I worked in a drugstore."

"What else did you do?"

"I shook hands with a seal once."

Margaret Werner laughed. "How perfectly marvelous," she said. "But really, haven't you ever done anything but work in a drugstore?"

"I danced naked on the Navy Pier."

"That's not very likely. For a glib person, you're really very reserved. Do you want to know my honest impression of you?"

"No," I said.

"That's not a very normal reaction."

"I'm as normal as the next one," I said, edging closer until our legs touched. "To look at you up there in the dress section at Finley's, who would have thought you were the kind of a girl that would be willing to sit on a rock with a fellow she hardly knew."

"I'm afraid I'm not what you'd call the smooching type," said the blond, getting up and brushing off her slacks.

"I knew all along you were out of my class."

"Oh pish! I hate people with inferiority complexes. Will you take me home?"

"Why not? It's on my way."

"Don't be nasty, darling. Have you ever read *Alice in*

Wonderland? Because I intend to read it to you someday. Tell me one thing more. Do you enjoy living with your grandmother?"

"Where else could I live?"

"Yes, where else?" she said as I helped her down from the rock. "Do you want to know something, darling? I like you. But I'm beginning to hate your grandmother."

The two-flat building on Wilton Avenue was much too big for us, Mabel said. If my grandmother ever intended to sell, the time to do it was before prices went down any farther. What the three of us needed according to Mabel was a little one-story cottage in a quiet neighborhood where my grandmother could get away from the noise of the elevated and wind up her days. My grandmother was in prime condition with no thought of winding up her days anywhere, but Mabel harped on the subject so long my grandmother decided it might be a good idea after all, only where could she find a cottage like the one Mabel described. Mabel practically brought the cottage home with her the next day. The husband of one of her clients was a real estate agent it turned out. The following Sunday she took my grandmother out to look at it.

"How was it?" I said when they got home.

"Why, it was very nice," said my grandmother. "I still think it's a little close to the tracks, Mabel."

"I thought you wanted to get away from the elevated," I said.

"Charlie, you have no right to influence your grandmother against the idea," said Mabel. "They aren't elevated tracks anyway. They're train tracks. Just think, Amanda, being able to lie in bed at night and listen to train whistles. I never did see such a cozy little cottage. Next summer we can plant vines all around it."

My grandmother finally agreed to buy the cottage but first she had to sell the two-flat house on Wilton Avenue and that took a little doing in those days. Mabel had already arranged that I was to sleep in the dining room of the new house next to the coal stove so that I could see the fire didn't go out in the middle of the night. I was to become Mabel's janitor just like my grandmother had become her maid. I didn't like the idea at all, but one wet September day when I was taking a load of bed jackets up to the seventh floor at Finley and Dunlap's I bumped into Maggie Werner and the problem solved itself.

"You've been avoiding me," she said. "You haven't forgotten I'm going to read *Alice in Wonderland* to you, have you? How about tonight? You can buy me a dinner. I'm broke."

"I don't have any money either."

"Then borrow some. You're not going to escape me that easily."

I didn't see much point in going out with a blond whose knees froze as soon as they touched yours, but after all I owed her a dinner so I borrowed seventy-five cents from Richard. It was all he could spare.

It was raining when we got out at five-thirty so we decided to eat downtown. The cheapest restaurant in the Loop was Alexander's on Clark Street where I had lunch with Richard sometimes on payday. Three dusty wax oranges on green doilies were lined up in the window against a stained-glass background that spelled out the name

ALEXANDER. It was not a very inviting place to take a girl but you could get complete dinners there, twenty-five and thirty cents, none higher. Margaret Werner had never heard of Alexander's. She thought it was very quaint until a man sat down at our table and began eating a corned beef sandwich the way an ordinary person would play "Nola" on the harmonica. "You may not know it," she said, "but I'm paying you a great compliment by dining with you in a dive like this."

We were quite soaked when we got to the house on Oakenwald but there was a fire going in the fireplace. Margaret Werner went upstairs to put on some dry clothes, leaving me alone with Mrs. O'Reilly, her landlady, an aging Irishwoman with red hair that always seemed to have a pencil or two sticking out of it. When Mrs. O'Reilly was seventeen, she had gone to work behind the notion counter at Finley and Dunlap's. During the First World War they put her in the information booth and she had been there ever since. Her favorite subjects of conversation were money and Margaret Werner. When I mentioned it was hot in the room she said, "Margaret likes it warm so I keep the house as hot as possible when she's home. Why don't you take off your jacket?"

"I better not. If I'd known I was going out tonight, I would have put on a clean shirt."

"If your shirt is dirty I'll wash it for your. Mr. O'Reilly used to say I did his shirts better than the Chinese laundry."

"Thanks just the same. You have a nice place here," I said to take the conversation off my shirt. Mrs. O'Reilly agreed it was a nice place.

"And it's handy to the lake in the summertime. Why, the very night Margaret moved in, do you know what she did?"

"She went swimming naked," I said.

"She really did. That girl fears nothing. And gentlemen friends! I can't keep track of them all. Margaret doesn't buy her own dinner one night out of seven. Some of her friends are worth a great deal of money. You're a stockboy, aren't you? You didn't strike me as the well-to-do type. Take Margaret now. You can tell she was worth a great deal when her father was alive. She's got a head on her too. You'd be surprised at the number of people who come into Finley's and won't let anyone on the seventh floor wait on them but Margaret. She has wonderful taste, that's why they keep coming back. Here she is now," said Mrs. O'Reilly, as Margaret Werner came down the steps in a padded housecoat that looked like a relic of better days. There was a book under her arm. "I was just telling your new young man what a flair you have for clothes."

"Why not? I wear them all the time."

Mrs. O'Reilly buried her face in her hands and laughed until a pencil fell out of her hair.

"Isn't she marvelous?" said Miss Werner, sitting down beside me on the sofa. "What have you two old maids been gabbing about?"

"Mr. Flowers thinks it's hot. He won't take his coat off because his shirt is dirty. I offered to wash it for him but he won't take it off."

"Not everyone can have their shirts done by Mrs. O. Go ahead, darling, take it off." I held my ground for a few minutes but between the two of them they got my shirt off and Mrs. O'Reilly disappeared with it into the kitchen. Margaret Werner kicked off her mules, hoisted her legs off the floor, and put her feet in my lap.

"Hey, what kind of a house is this?" I said.

She smiled and said, "Give me a cigarette." I gave her one and tried not to touch her bare leg when I held the match.

"I wish you'd let me put my coat on."

"You look very nice the way you are. And stop blushing. I despise bashful people."

Before I could think of anything to say, Mrs. O'Reilly flounced out of the kitchen with the shirt. It didn't look any cleaner than before, just wetter. She draped it over a corner of the fire screen and said, "Why don't you read to us, Margaret? *Alice in Wonderland* would be nice. Margaret reads that to everybody," she added, picking up a pencil stub from the floor and putting it in her hair. Then she scattered a handful of colored salts on the fire from a box on the mantel. The logs in the fireplace sizzled, the flames changed color, red, green, blue and yellow. Margaret Werner opened the book.

"Alice in Wonderland. Chapter One. Down the Rabbit Hole."

The book was for children. I spent an uncomfortable hour listening to it, keeping one eye on my shirt in case it caught fire and the other on the long naked leg that Margaret Werner kept swinging in front of me. After an hour she grew tired of the sound of her own voice and passed the book to Mrs. O'Reilly who read a chapter and passed the book to me. While Mrs. O'Reilly set the ironing board up in front of the fireplace, I read a page, then I closed the book and Margaret Werner suggested I come upstairs and look at her room. "Will the old lady mind?" I said on the stairs.

"Mrs. O mind? Of course not. She's a born match-maker."

Miss Werner's room was on the third floor and had a table with a heavy gold lamp, a chaise lounge with broken springs, and a box mattress bed supported on bricks. "Now I'll show you Mr. Matthews' room," she said. Mr. Matthews was a musician who worked as a shoe salesman at Finley's. His room looked out over the IC tracks to the lake. "It has a nice view, but he's never in it long enough to appreciate the view," she went on. "He spends half his spare time down-town practicing on his tuba. The other half he spends in the bathroom. That's why I'm late to work so often. We share the bath up here."

"How much does a room like this cost?"

"Five dollars a week but there's a vacant room on the second floor for four dollars. Speaking of rooms, when are you going to break away from your grandmother's apron strings and become independent?"

"Four dollars is a lot of money. It's different with you, Maggie. You make more money than me."

"Do you have to call me Maggie?"

"I won't if you don't want me to."

"Don't be so damned obliging. As a matter of fact it sounds rather smart."

"Can I call you Maggie then?"

"I'll tell you a secret, darling. Nobody else could. People either bore me or they amuse me. Mrs. O amuses me. So do you, but it goes deeper than that. I'm what you might call an amateur psychologist. I like to get to the bottom of people and find out what makes them tick. That's what I'm trying to find out about you. Hasn't it occurred to you why I invited you here tonight?"

"To read me a book?"

"Don't be gullible. Besides, you didn't listen to a word of it. I thought you might be interested in moving into that room on the second floor."

"If I moved in, would I have a chance with you?"

"Don't be obvious," she said, shoving my arm away. "You're different from the others. Stay that way, darling."

When I woke up the next morning, my grandmother was standing in the middle of the kitchen, holding up my shirt with the marks of Mrs. O'Reilly's fire screen across the back of it and a big scorch mark on the tail. I explained I was out with Richard the night before and spilled catsup on my shirt so his mother washed and ironed it for me. "She's a widow," I added for good measure.

"So am I a widow," said my grandmother. "But I don't go around burning up other people's shirts. You make her pay for it or buy you a new one, do you hear?"

I heard so much about Richard's mother and the spoiled shirt in the next few days I decided that maybe it was time to leave home and move into Mrs. O'Reilly's and become independent after all. The first time I mentioned it, my grandmother refused to discuss it. It was out of the question, she said. I was still a minor. Then a month later she sold the house on Wilton Avenue and got ready to move so I brought the subject up again. My grandmother offered me her bedroom in the new house in exchange for staying. The third time I brought the subject up, she cried.

"Don't leave me, Charlie. You're all I have."

"I'll come out and have dinner with you and Mabel once a week," I said, staring out the window at the elevated tracks. I didn't have the nerve to tell her that the real reason I was moving was that I was in love with Maggie Werner and couldn't help it.

SEVEN

The way I pictured life at Mrs. O'Reilly's, Maggie would sit beside me in front of the fireplace every night, our knees touching, while Mrs. O'Reilly talked about money and every now and then got up to throw a handful of magic salts on the fire, but the way it turned out, there was never a fire in the fireplace unless Maggie was home and Maggie was almost never home.

Mrs. O'Reilly was always home. Every night I had to listen to what went on at the information booth that day. When Mrs. O'Reilly got tired of talking about Finley and

Dunlap's, she would talk about money and when she got tired of talking about money she would talk about her house, which had several mortgages hanging over it like thunderstorms. Before I moved in, I took it for granted she was a widow. She wasn't. The reason Mr. O'Reilly was never mentioned was that he didn't work any more but lived in the kitchen and took tonic to keep alive. The tonic was alcoholic.

The only person in that house who was well-off was Mr. Matthews, the shoe salesman from Finley's. One night Maggie knocked on my door and said I should come upstairs and listen to *The Firebird* on Mr. Matthews' record player. Maggie had her own ideas about everything. It was her idea we should sit on the floor and smoke Mr. Matthews' cigarettes while the music went on and on and the tubes in the record player cast a yellow glow against Mrs. O'Reilly's faded third-floor wallpaper. "It's long for being just about a firebug," I said.

"Doesn't he say the cleverest things?" said Maggie. Mr. Matthews grunted. Maggie slipped her hand into mine in the dark and let me fiddle with her fingers. When the music was over she invited us into her room to try out her new percolator. Mr. Matthews bowed out but I followed Maggie into the front bedroom. She shut the door and plugged in the percolator. Then she poured us each a cup and draped herself on the sagging chaise lounge. "Sit here," she said, moving over. She put her cup on the table and lay looking at me with her lips parted a little. I brought my head closer, then my lips just naturally slipped on top of hers.

"What happened?" I said, coming up for air.

"I've finally made up my mind about you," she said, letting me kiss her again. Making up for lost time, I slipped one hand under her back. My other hand slipped down around the region of her legs. She pushed it away. I put it back. She pushed it away again and sat up so suddenly I slid off onto the floor. "Look here," she said, sounding hurt. "I'm not a common prostitute. On the other hand I'm not a prude. My God, you don't think me a prude, do you?"

"You mean this is as far as it goes?"

"Must you be so explicit? There's only one thing that stands between thee and me, darling. You don't have any money."

"I don't see what money has to do with it."

"Don't you? If you had any guts you'd go up to the ninth floor tomorrow and ask for a raise or get out of Finley's and find a decent job. You're stupid not to."

"OK, so I'm stupid. They'd only fire me."

"Damn it, darling, you're not stupid. Compared to you, most of the people I know are damned dull. There ought to be something you'd be good at. I'd like to see you when you're really loosened up. Frankly, I don't think you've ever been decently drunk or been to a decent party or slept with a decent girl in your life. You're very attractive when you blush," she said, kissing my ear. "Will you go with me to a party Saturday night? The Alpha Tau's are having a blowout."

"What would I be doing in a frat house?"

"Fraternity house, darling. Nobody says frat at the university."

Maggie made all the arrangements. She had a friend named Erica who drove a Nash. Erica's brother lived in a

96

fraternity house on Woodlawn Avenue. It turned out he was taking Maggie, I was supposed to be taking Erica. Erica was something of a stick but there was plenty of bathtub gin to make up for it. All the drinking was done in the kitchen. I had several, then I went in the other room to look for Maggie. They had a pretty good band in there and it wasn't long before that old feeling began to ripple back into my bones. It was like the first time I looked out the window of my grandmother's attic and saw the twinkling lights of the Melody Gardens spread out below. This was the chance I had been waiting for all my life. I started off with the first routine Mr. Barney ever taught me. After that it was like I was breaking loose from my moorings or something. Everything went all right until I tried to take a bow and fell into a tray of sandwiches. The last thing I remember was being poured into the Nash by about six people. I was paralyzed at last.

Sunday I slept all day. When I got up at four-thirty, Maggie was in her room, reading.

"Can I come in?"

"It looks as if you're already in," she said without looking up.

"Are you mad at me?"

"Not mad. Merely disappointed."

"OK, so I got drunk," I said. "So did everyone else."

"They didn't get stinking. Smart people drink. They don't get drunk. Oh darling," she said, closing the book, "I have never seen anything like it. I've seen half-baked sophomores who had a small part in Blackfriars get tight and show off at a party as if they thought they were Bill Robinson. But you, of all people! You didn't know when to stop.

Sit down and give me a cigarette. I want to ask you a few questions. Have you ever read any Freud?" she said, tapping the cigarette on the book. "If you had, you'd understand what I mean when I say you're a beautiful case of arrested development."

"I never got arrested."

"Don't be idiotic. What happened last night didn't happen by accident. It was the result of something that happened to you when you were a child."

"I think it was the gin."

"On the contrary, darling. It was probably that grandmother of yours. She kept you in short pants too long. Grandmothers do those things."

"Not mine. You should meet the old bag."

"I intend to," said Maggie. "You have dinner with her once a week. I'm going with you next time."

My grandmother's cozy cottage, as Mabel called it, was a small one-story house on the Southwest Side, jammed in between a dead-end street and the CB&Q railroad tracks. The only decent-sized room was Mabel's. I did my best to keep Maggie out of the conversation when I ate dinner there but she kept creeping into it along with Mr. Matthews and Listerine Annie and Mrs. O'Reilly.

"I told you there was a woman behind all this," said Mabel.

"Why shouldn't there be?" said my grandmother, trying hard to hide her pride. "It's time Charlie had a girl. Why don't you bring her out for dinner some night?"

I made excuses because I was ashamed of Mabel and my grandmother and their crowded little house, but when

Maggie practically invited herself I couldn't put it off any longer. There was nothing to fear it turned out. My grandmother was on her best behavior. So was Maggie. She offered to help in the kitchen but my grandmother wouldn't hear of it. Mabel came in a few minutes later, looking like something that had been walking the streets for twenty-five years without anybody making a pass at it. "So you're Charlie's new girl," she said, putting her hands on her hips. "You could do with a little fattening. So could most of the girls who work at Finley's. I think Finley's is the most refined store in Chicago but I don't flatter myself I can afford to shop there."

"I don't buy there either," said Maggie. "I think their clothes are atrocious."

"Well!" said Mabel. "You're the first person I ever heard say that."

When we sat down at the table, my grandmother announced out of a clear sky, "I will now say grace. You know, Miss Werner, Pastor Froelich used to say Charlie was the most religious boy in the Sunday school at one time."

"How nice," said Maggie. "You never told me, darling."

My grandmother shot Mabel a quick glance at the word darling, then she stumbled through grace for the first time in ten years.

The dinner was a big success. When we were halfway through, Mabel and my grandmother got in an argument over some horses that were running down in Florida. Mabel had put fifty cents for each of them on a horse that day and here it was eight o'clock and the horse hadn't come in yet. I couldn't help laughing myself. Maggie was in hysterics.

"Whatever you say about my judgment, Amanda, you've got to admit if it hadn't been for me you would have lost your pants in the stock market," said Mabel, glancing at Maggie for approval.

"You're right, Mabel. You know, Miss Werner, Mabel made me put everything I had left in a safe deposit box. Even if the bank goes broke, it will still be there. Enough to bury me anyway."

"She's been dying ever since she had her gallstones out but she'll last longer than any of us. That poor woman used to slave day in, day out, running a boarding house, until I came along and showed her there were easier ways of making money than turning yourself into a drudge. For heaven's sake, Amanda, what's the matter?"

My grandmother had covered her face with her hands. She was laughing. "Oh my!" she said finally. "I was just thinking about the time Charlie took his grandfather's ashes out of the bookcase. I haven't thought of that in years."

"It wasn't me. It was Stinko."

"Stinko!" screamed Maggie. She made my grandmother tell her all about it. Then she threw back her head and howled.

"Mr. Slaughter was a fine man," said my grandmother, wiping her eyes, "but I got tired of seeing him on the mantel and put him in the bookcase."

"I don't blame her one little bit," cut in Mabel. "I get so tired of men I could scream."

Before we left, Maggie went in the bathroom. Mabel trailed along after her. I put on my coat and sat down by the stove and thanked my grandmother for fixing such a good dinner.

"I enjoyed it, Charlie. I'd hate to tell you what I spent on that steak. Mabel will never let me forget it."

"It's your money."

"Well, I ought to know enough by now not to bother you with my troubles," said my grandmother with a sigh. "Yes, it was a nice dinner. I haven't had such a good time in years. Maggie's a fine girl. She'll make you a fine wife."

"Oh for God sake," I said, "nobody's getting married. She just wanted to meet you, that's all."

While we were waiting for the streetcar, Maggie said, "Now I know where your sense of humor comes from. Your grandmother is terribly funny. So is Mabel. She's the type of person that would wear perfume to a picnic. Do you know why she followed me into the bathroom? She wanted me to try some of her rouge. She thought I looked consumptive."

"Did you?"

"But darling, nobody wears rouge any more. What you know about women could be written on the head of a pin." We got off the streetcar downtown and took the IC electric from there. Maggie didn't say anything until we got to 39th Street, then she said, "Does your grandmother really have money? Because if she does, it could be the saving of you. If she died and left you a halfway decent sum, you could quit that lousy job of yours and do something. I can't imagine what."

"Say, I never thought of that. I suppose if my grandmother died and left me a million dollars you'd marry me."

"But darling, how perfectly ridiculous," said Maggie. "Of course I would."

That was the worst year of the depression for Finley and Dunlap's. They didn't want to fire anybody so they thought up a plan. Everyone would take one day off a week, then they would only have to pay us for five days instead of six. The plan worked fine until Christmas shopping began, then service became so bad that they worked out a brand-new plan. Everybody would go back to working six days a week, and it wouldn't cost anybody a cent because we would still be paid for only five days.

As if that wasn't tricky enough, they began firing people one at a time. Mrs. McHallam, who had spent forty years in bedspreads and whose pension was due in six months, got fired so they wouldn't have to pay her pension. A floorwalker on the eighth floor was the last person to see her alive. One minute she was running her hand along the marble railing at the top of the famous stairway under the stained-glass dome, looking over the railing at the fountain on the main floor. The next minute she was gone.

Mrs. McHallam missed the fountain by ten feet, hitting one of the notion counters where a saleslady who had worked at Finley's for only nineteen years was standing, and both of them were killed. Mrs. O'Reilly, who had known both the dead women, was filling the fireplace with tears when we got home. That was too much for Maggie.

"We're a bunch of damned fools," she said. "We let them walk all over us down at the store and they'll go right on doing it unless we get together and stop them."

"But what can we do?" I said.

"We can't bring back Mrs. McHallam but we can all get together and form a union," said Maggie.

Unions were mostly for carpenters in those days but

Maggie had been to college and knew all the answers. She got some salesladies on the seventh floor interested and made Mr. Albertson talk to the floorwalkers on the other floors. Then she told me to organize the stockboys. I didn't know how to go about it and was quite relieved when Richard took the whole business out of my hands. He had the same idea all along and the following day he had lunch with Maggie. Within two days they were collecting dues. Within a week they rented a vacant store on Lake Street and held a meeting.

Almost a hundred people showed up. Maggie climbed on a packing case and made a speech with her head thrown back like Joan of Arc, then Richard made a speech. He said he had been investigating and found there was already a union for department store workers and he would get in touch with them and let us know. Two days later he began signing people up in a real union. By the week before Christmas more than a hundred employees had joined. They decided to take the Monday before Christmas off and parade up and down in front of the store with signs. All anybody talked about Saturday was what was going to happen Monday when the union members pulled out.

When Maggie came home that night she took her shoes off and sat down in front of the fireplace. She was going to talk turkey, she said. If a one-day strike would help she was all for it, but personally she thought we ought to wait until after Christmas.

"We have to strike while the iron is hot," I said.

"That's what you said at the meeting, Margaret," said Mrs. O'Reilly.

"I'm just being practical. It stands to reason that anyone who takes part in that monkey business Monday will be cutting his own throat. The ninth floor isn't going to take this lying down."

"But the ninth floor is scared," I said. "Only this morning they offered Richard a raise but he turned it down."

"If Richard wants to make a martyr out of himself, that's his business. I was called up to the ninth floor myself, by the way. I had a long talk with Mr. Henderson."

"Mr. Henderson!" gasped Mrs. O'Reilly. "What did he say?"

"Frankly, I was surprised. He seems to understand a great deal more about our troubles than we do ourselves. He says the younger men on the ninth floor have what you might call a union too. They're anxious to take over from the fuddy-duddies and really modernize Finley's. He also said they appreciated the fine work I've been doing and offered me a raise. Two dollars a week. My God! I laughed in his face. But he was very decent about it. He took me out to Henrici's for lunch afterwards."

"Henrici's!" screamed Mrs. O'Reilly.

"But you're the brains behind the union," I said.

"I was until your friend Richard took over. Listen, darling, you're not seriously thinking of joining that bunch of wild men and going off half-cocked Monday, are you?"

"I promised Richard."

"A two-dollar raise!" bubbled Mrs. O'Reilly. "That's twenty a week and you haven't been there three years yet. I think that's wonderful."

"It's less than half of what I'm worth."

"You mean you accepted the raise? I said.

"Of course," said Maggie. "What do you take me for, darling? A fool?"

If I ever wanted to walk up and down State Street with a sign, I didn't now. But a promise was a promise and Richard was my friend. I showed up Monday morning in the alley alongside Finley's. There were only about thirty of us, all men except for Listerine Annie who had never been a union member but was a little cracked anyway. At a quarter of eight we began marching up and down with signs. I carried a little one that said REMEMBER MRS. McHALLAM—as if she had been a battleship like the *Maine*. I didn't see anything wrong with that.

People on their way to work frowned. Some of them smiled. At eight o'clock Mr. Henderson passed through the revolving doors, looking at his watch. Then fifteen minutes before the store was supposed to open, a parade of mounted policemen came down State Street from the direction of the Boston Store. They were riding two abreast and their horses were blowing steam. At the same time, another army of policemen came marching around the corner with their nightsticks out. Richard stood his ground but the rest of us dropped our signs and didn't stop running until we got to Clark Street. I sat in Alexander's with another stockboy for an hour, drinking coffee. Then we went back to Finley's. Mr. Nelson told us if we were looking for Richard we wouldn't find him there. He was in the hospital. Then he sent us up to the ninth floor where we were given our pay and fired for coming late to work.

That was the worst time of year to look for a job. I didn't know what to do. The only thing I wouldn't do was go back to my grandmother's. On Thanksgiving Mabel had got into a fight with me over which end of the turkey I was entitled to and I hadn't been back since. My money ran out New Year's and I spent the day in a blue mood. "Look, darling," said Maggie, "if you're going to carry on like a widow with a funeral bill, I'll go crazy. I've just had an idea. I spend fifty cents for dinner when I don't have a date. I'll give you fifty cents a day and we can both eat for the price of one. You can buy the food and prepare it on the gas ring in the bathroom."

"That won't pay the rent."

"A vacant room won't pay the janitor. Mrs. O pays a man seven dollars a month to take care of the furnace. If you take over the furnace, she can let the janitor go and you can forget about room rent until you get a job. I've already spoken to her about it and she thinks it's a perfectly wonderful arrangement. There's only one other thing. Can you cook?"

She soon found out. Food was cheap in those days. The first night we had pork chops but they got done too fast. The next night it was lamb patties. They were better but Maggie didn't show up until everything was cold. The night after that it was hamburgers. Maggie had a date that night and didn't show up at all so I took the hamburgers down to the O'Reillys who declared they were delicious.

Toward the end of February I got desperate and answered an ad to sell wine bricks from door to door. Maggie loaned me five dollars and I bought a box of bricks that were supposed to be soaked in water. The water would then turn into wine like in the Bible. At the end of two weeks I had sold one brick and my shoes needed resoling so I gave the rest of the bricks to Mr. O'Reilly to use for tonic.

The O'Reillys were having troubles of their own. Mrs. O'Reilly lived in constant fear of getting fired before her pension came due, like Mrs. McHallam. She decided to go into the rooming house business in a big way that summer so she took a month's vacation without pay and scraped together enough money to buy paint for the second floor. I painted it for her. She hung a TOURISTS sign in the window and turned the whole second floor into a tourist trap but if anyone made money that summer it wasn't Mrs. O'Reilly. She went back to work a week before her month was up, red around the eyes from weeping so much.

On Labor Day Maggie drove up to Wisconsin with her friend Erica for a week's vacation. While she was gone I lay on the rocks at the foot of 47th Street and watched the mist roll in off the lake like it sometimes did in September and listened to the foghorns thumping away on the five-mile cribs. I didn't even go through the motions of looking for work until the day after Maggie came home. Then I walked all the way downtown, needing the exercise as much as I needed to save the money.

On my way up Clark Street I almost passed Alexander's without recognizing it. The wall of the vacant store next door had been knocked down so the restaurant was twice as large as before. The dusty oranges in the window were gone forever along with the pancakes and coffee for ten cents and the twenty-five-cent dinners. Now I always had a soft spot in my heart for the old Alexander's. You can say what you want about the food they served but it kept a lot of people from starving in those days and it made me sad to think that Alexander's had become just another self-service lunchroom with a basket of funeral flowers in the window to announce the grand opening. The flowers were already beginning to wilt. Leaning against the bottom of the basket was a sign: DISHWASHER WANTED.

Long ago when I first started washing dishes for my grandmother, I formed the idea that dishwashing was the bottom of the ladder. Times had changed. "See the manager," said the cashier and pointed to a door against the back wall. As soon as I pushed open that door I had one of those blinding flashes that are supposed to come over you when you drown. Everything that had happened to me from the monkey suit on down whizzed past my eyes and came to an end in a dishwasher's job in the kitchen of Alexander's—as if that was the break I had been waiting for all my life.

The manager was crouched over a desk in the corner. I couldn't believe my eyes. Alexander's new manager was my old friend Mr. Barney. He didn't look up at first so I did a couple of riffs over to the desk, then I wound up with my snappiest break.

"Well I'll be a horse's banana, if it isn't Charlie Flowers."

"Who did you think it was," I said, "the King of Siam?"

I hurried home and opened a can of hash and boiled a couple of potatoes on the gas ring in the bathroom. Maggie was late for dinner and out of sorts so I decided to wait until she was in a better humor before breaking the news.

She took a forkful of hash and a bite of soggy potato and said, "Really, this is too nauseating." Then she lit a cigarette and sat down on the chaise lounge. I went on eating.

"I did a lot of thinking about you while I was on my vacation," she said. "You don't want to work. That's your trouble. You're incurable."

"How can I be incurable? I was never even sick."

"Oh stop acting like a pet monkey. I get so tired of that pose."

I went right on eating.

"I'm sorry," she said after a minute. "This is so silly. Let's kiss and make up. It's not good for you to go on this way."

I wiped my mouth and went over to the chaise lounge and kissed her. "That's the way I feel," I said. "What good does kissing do if it never goes any farther? It's like making love to a stone wall."

"That isn't what I mean," said Maggie, getting mad. "You know very well what I mean. I mean you haven't looked for work in weeks and weeks. Mrs. O said you didn't go downtown once the whole time I was in Wisconsin. You're never going to find a job if you don't look for one. You've given up."

"That's a lie. I can prove it."

Maggie got up and snuffed out her cigarette in the hash. "Some other time. I'm in a terrible hurry. I have a date."

"Well, don't let me keep you," I said. I gathered up the dishes and carried them into the bathroom and slammed them into the sink, breaking a cup in the process. Then I went downstairs and packed my bag and carried it down to the telephone closet under the stairs and called my grandmother.

"Oh Charlie," she said when she heard my voice. "The least you could have done was let me know you were alive."

"The reason I didn't call was I lost my job," I explained. "Now I've got a new one and I'm coming home."

"I'll have to ask Mabel. She's not home yet."

"Whose house is it, yours or Mabel's?" I said and hung up.

When I came out of the closet under the stairs, Mrs. O'Reilly was sitting in front of the fireplace, scratching her head with a pencil and humming to herself in that terrible intent way people have who have been listening to somebody else's telephone conversation.

"I suppose you heard," I said. "I got a job washing dishes but it only pays ten dollars a week so I'm going home."

"Oh dear," said Mrs. O'Reilly, sticking the pencil back in her hair. "I always said there could never be anything between you and Margaret. Her other friends are worth such a lot of money." Then she stopped as if she was shocked at the sound of her own words. "I meant that in a nice way, Mr. Flowers," she said. "It's for your own good."

"Everything always is," I said. "Good-bye, Mrs. O'Reilly." It wasn't until I got on the streetcar that I realized what I was leaving behind—the long legs, the tricky blond hair, the way Maggie had of saying darling with every other word as if it was more important to her than breathing. And when I thought of what I was leaving behind there was a bitter taste in my mouth and a tight feeling at the back of my throat like I wanted to cry.

EIGHT

In my grandmother's new house I slept on a cot next to the coal stove in the dining room. It was the warmest spot in the house as Mabel pointed out. Mabel was in her element in that cluttered house, but when my grandmother talked about the flat on Wilton Avenue she grew almost as sad as she once did when she talked about the boardinghouse next to the Melody Gardens. We had come a long way since then, mostly down, but my grandmother had developed a good soul in her old age. She fed me pretty well. Mabel had a new boyfriend, a seventy-year-old lawyer, and she went out more. When she got home she would rummage around the icebox and come in the living room, gnawing a cold pork chop and say, "I declare, Amanda, since Charlie moved back, there's never anything to eat in this house."

Mabel never spoke to me direct any more. She got in the habit of speaking to me through my grandmother as if I was in the other room.

"What's Charlie going to do? Sit around the house all day on his day off? Doesn't he have any girl friends?"

"Well, he had a nice one, Mabel. I wouldn't be surprised if he made it up with Maggie someday."

"That bag of bones! I never saw such skinny legs in my life."

I wound up going to an average of three movies a week, just to get away from Mabel. But I rose fast at Alexander's, thanks to Mr. Barney, and that made up for a lot of things.

Mr. Barney had never gone to Brazil. What happened was he got a job with a South American coffee company in Chicago after getting kicked out of his old studio on Randolph Street for not paying the rent. When the coffee company folded up, a friend of his in show business opened a restaurant on the Near North Side and gave him a job as a waiter. When Alexander's expanded, his friend happened to know Mr. Alexander so Mr. Barney got the job as manager.

To get a job in those days you had to have a friend. Mr. Barney was my friend and under his watchful eye I did OK. After two weeks I was promoted to odd jobs like working the bread slicer. Within two months I was a full-fledged busboy and before long was doubling for the countermen when they failed to show up. Six months after I came to work at Alexander's one of the countermen went on a binge that lasted four days. By the time he came back I had his job.

One night that spring a lady came into Alexander's and asked for a cup of coffee. I was glad I had on a clean white jacket and that my cap was tilted at the proper angle because when I looked up, it was Maggie. She was wearing her hair long that year. It looked like liquid honey.

"Without cream, darling. You know I take it black. Why don't you take off that silly cap and sit down and have a cigarette with me?"

"We're too busy."

"When do they let you out of this awful place?"

"Seven o'clock."

"I'll wait for you then."

Now that prohibition was over, there were several new taverns in the Loop that sold wine and beer. At seven o'clock I took Maggie to a tavern around the corner on Madison Street, where they served beer in thick mugs with heavy glass bottoms. Maggie sat down and helped herself to a pretzel. "Do you remember that sordid place above the Blackhawk?" she said. "And that yeasty brew?"

"That was where I made my first mistake," I said, "letting you pay for it. How did you find out I was working at Alexander's?"

"There's a depraved element at Finley's that insists on eating in such places. It was just a matter of time until the news reached Mrs. O'Reilly and the information booth. Mrs. O's been fired you know. From the store's standpoint she was becoming quite impossible. They're modernizing the place from top to bottom. They put in new elevators last fall."

"It sounds as if you like the place."

"I never disliked Finley's. It was the old guard I didn't like. If it hadn't been for Mr. Henderson, I'd have left ages ago. But I do get bored. People have bored me for a whole year, darling. You're like a breath of fresh air. Do you suppose I'm drunk?"

"You've only had one."

"Don't you think we'd better have another?"

"That might be a good idea." When the beer came I said, "What did you really come to see me about?"

"I won't lie to you," said Maggie. "It's about Mrs. O. Her taxes are so far in arrears she's afraid the house will be sold from under her. Last week Mr. Matthews got a job in an orchestra in Minneapolis and moved away. It's hard on Mrs. O with two rooms vacant and no salary coming in." She took a sip of beer and reached for my hand under the bar. I put it in my pocket. "Really, darling, you've sulked long enough. It must be very amusing living with Mabel and your grandmother, but enough is enough. Why don't you move back to Mrs. O's?"

"Would it make any difference between you and me?"

"You drive a hard bargain," said Maggie. "Why don't you try it and see?"

When I broke the news to my grandmother, she didn't say anything. She just poured us each a cup of coffee and set the pot on the kitchen table. For some reason it reminded me of that night long ago when she and my father sat at the table in the dining room of the old boardinghouse with a pot of coffee between them. I could still hear her saying, "You can't leave him with me, Henry Flowers," and my father saying, "Now Amanda, not in front of the boy."

"I won't say I'm surprised and I won't say I'm not," said my grandmother finally. "I won't try to stop you, Charlie. This house never lived up to your expectations, or mine either."

"It isn't the house," I said. "It's Mabel."

"It isn't Mabel," said my grandmother. "It's Maggie."

"It isn't Maggie," I said. "It's Mrs. O'Reilly. She can't pay her taxes without another roomer."

"I have taxes to pay too."

"Oh for God sake, let's not argue about it."

"No, we won't argue about it," said my grandmother. "I've done a lot of things in my life I shouldn't have done. I'm too old to change now but maybe I can make things up to you when I die."

"You shouldn't talk like that. You'll live forever."

"We all have to go someday. When I die, I want you to have the diamonds. They're all paid for now. They'd make a nice present for Maggie when you decide to get married. It will be a fine match. She'll make something of you, Charlie."

"You don't know what you're talking about. Maggie doesn't mean anything to me. Anyway she doesn't wear jewelry."

"Then you could pass them on to your children. I'd like you to have the house too but I know how you feel about that. It's not like when we lived next door to the Melody Gardens."

"Now let's not get off on the subject of the old days," I

said. "And thanks for the diamonds. I'll let you give them to me when I get married."

"I didn't say when you got married," snapped my grandmother. "I said when I die."

"OK," I said. "When you die."

After that it was just a matter of putting a few things into a bag and getting off the 47th Street streetcar at the end of the line.

Mrs. O'Reilly was glad to see me. "I couldn't afford to have Mr. Matthews' old room redecorated," she said, "but I moved the furniture around."

"It's a very manly room," said Maggie.

"What's the matter with my old room?" I said.

Mrs. O'Reilly pushed a pencil back in her thinning hair and said, "Margaret thought you'd be happier up here."

I didn't argue. I carried my suitcase into the back room and got into my pajamas. Maggie knocked on the bathroom door while I was brushing my teeth. "I fixed some coffee," she said. "I hope you don't mind drinking it black."

When I came out of the bathroom she was stretched out on the chaise lounge in her old housecoat with a cup and saucer beside her. I sat down on the edge of the bed with a cup of coffee, feeling almost naked in my pajamas.

"Am I boring you?" said Maggie after a minute.

"No," I said. "Am I boring you?"

"You're the first man that never has. Is it because I've never been able to figure you out?"

"What is there to figure out?"

"Look here, darling, you're not trying to make a damn fool out of me, are you? Like the time you let me bawl you out for not looking for a job when you already had one?"

"Did I make a fool out of you?"

"Yes you did. I'm not so sure you're not doing it now. But at the moment I don't happen to care."

"Most people if they want to make fools out of themselves—just leave them alone and they'll do it," I said.

"Are you quite sure you didn't take a course in psychology somewhere along the line, darling? Let's stop this nonsense. Come over here and kiss me."

"I'll be damned first," I said. "You come over here."

Maggie was a complete virgin it turned out. Nobody was more surprised than me.

Moving back to Mrs. O'Reilly's was like being born all over again into a world of springtime and double beds and long-legged blonds. Maggie went out with other men as often as ever but none of them shared the third-floor bath with her like me. When Mr. Barney gave me another raise that spring I could afford to take her downtown once or twice a month myself.

Maggie pretended to be an authority on jazz. I never cared for it myself, being the sentimental type. "It can't hold a candle to the music that used to come floating over the wall of the Melody Gardens next to my grandmother's boardinghouse," I said one night.

"But darling, you never told me you lived next door to the Melody Gardens."

"That was years ago. They must be out of business by now."

"Far from it. Since beer and ale came back, they're considered rather smart. Be a lamb and take me when they open this summer."

We went the second week in July. All my life I thought the Melody Gardens were for other people. I was afraid that the doorman in the long green coat would turn us back at the last moment but he didn't and here we were sitting at a table under the rustling leaves and the swaying lanterns, drinking ale because Maggie claimed it was superior to beer. The bandstand with the little stage in front of it was still there and so was the runway coming down between the tables. Everything looked smaller than in the old days but there was an aroma to the Melody Gardens that all the fancy bars in the Loop could never hope to have.

The show wasn't so hot but it was pleasant to talk and drink ale between the acts and let your eyes roam around. There was a four-story apartment building on the other side of the wall where the boardinghouse once stood. On the top floor a fat lady was sitting on the back porch, fanning herself.

"What are you staring at?" said Maggie. "You look as if you'd just seen a ghost."

"I have," I said. Then all at once I found myself telling Maggie how I used to watch the show at the Melody Gardens from the attic window. I told her about the monkey suit and my father and the fake barrel organ, about Lucy Ives and the pier, about Mr. Barney and how I wanted to be a dancer and go on the stage. It bubbled and spurted out in all directions, none of it in the right order but it didn't matter. We were both a little drunk by that time. Maggie was as flushed and excited as if she just stumbled over a crock of old gold that had been lying at her feet for years.

"But darling, this is amazing. No wonder I've never understood you before. I didn't think you'd ever been inside a theater except to go to a movie. You're the most untheatrical person I know."

"That's the whole trouble," I said.

"But the effect is just the opposite. You have talent to burn. It oozes out of you in spite of yourself. It's in the way you move, the things you say. It's all there, bottled up inside of you. All it needs is an outlet. Of course I don't know anything about dancing, technically speaking, but there must be barrels of money in it. Let's have another ale and talk this thing through."

I signaled the waiter. He went by the table without stopping.

"I don't think of money in terms of barrels," I said. "Anyways, dancers aren't made, they're born. Like seals."

"Don't be like that, darling. Compared to those fat hams in the floor show, you're worth your weight in gold. You're loaded with talent. The trouble is you keep it hidden as if you were ashamed of it. You've got to learn to impress other people the way you impress me. Watch this. Hey, Herman!" she screamed. The waiter turned around. Maggie pointed to our empty glasses. The waiter smiled and held up two fingers.

"People never pay any attention to me," I said.

"Of course they don't. You've made up your mind in advance that you're inferior to other people. You're not." When the ale came, she tapped a cigarette on the edge of the table and said, "I have you fairly well figured out by now. You've had a morbid attachment for this place. For years you've thought the Melody Gardens were too good for you. In reality, it's the other way round. Look about you. Shaky tables, wormy bandstand, waiters with dirty aprons! Strictly third-rate. Nightclubs," she said, drawing on the cigarette while I held the light, "that's your field, m'boy. I don't pretend to be an authority on psychoanalysis but I've had enough psychology to know that you've had a fixation for this place for most of your life. Now it's over," she said, snapping her fingers. "You've told me about it. You've made a clean breast of it. You can go on from here."

"I'd have to start all over again," I said. "I'd have to take lessons."

"Then take lessons."

"With what?"

"Oh hell, I don't know. Quit smoking. Starve. Sometimes you exasperate me. Why must you make such a pretense of being stupid? You're not, you know. Look, love do you want my honest opinion of you? You're not only not stupid, you're clever. Damned clever."

"If I'm clever, you're drunk."

"That's not very likely," said Maggie. She got up and stood beside the table, swaying slightly on her high heels. "Remember this night. Someday when you're rich and famous, look back and remember—remember Maggie, the dowdy little shopgirl from Finley and Dunlap's, who set your feet on the road to success. And don't think I'm ever going to let you forget it," she said. "Think it over, darling. I have to go to the john."

Maybe Maggie was right. Maybe I still had a chance to do something and make something of my life. It was hard to believe, but it was also hard to believe I was sitting in the middle of the Melody Gardens waiting for a beautiful blond to come back from the toilet. If that could happen to me, anything could.

Time passes fast when you are happy. I hadn't seen my grandmother in six months or called her up in four. Then one night in November my conscience began to bother me and I gave her a ring. Nobody answered. The next night I called again. Mabel answered but hung up as soon as she heard my voice.

I was on the afternoon shift that week so I went out the next morning and found the house locked. An Italian family lived next door. I rang the bell. "Mrs. Slaughter died the first week in October," said the Italian lady, crossing herself. "She never set foot outside the house after you left."

"Doesn't Mabel still live there?"

"That one! She comes and she goes but she don't speak to nobody. The house is for sale but she can't find a buyer."

I called up Maggie from a drugstore and told her the news.

"I'm so awfully sorry," she said. "What's to become of the property?"

"What property?"

"The house, the diamonds, everything."

"I don't know. I haven't thought about it. Mabel isn't home."

"Then park on her doorstep until she gets home. Oh darling, I feel as if something tremendous were about to happen."

I didn't feel that way at all, I just felt numb. I went back to my grandmother's house and sat on the doorstep in the sunshine. A little after twelve a taxi pulled up and out stepped Mabel in a new fur coat. She threw her arms around me and kissed me. Clouds of perfume welled up from inside her coat.

"Oh Charlie, I'm so glad to see you. Your grandmother had a stroke and died in her sleep. I looked high and low for your address but I couldn't find it anywhere."

"You could have called Alexander's."

"Isn't that silly? It never occurred to me. How about some coffee?"

If the house looked like a mess in my grandmother's day, it looked like a pigpen now. The kitchen sink was clogged with dirty dishes and crusts of toast. "I can't offer you anything except coffee," explained Mabel. "I've been eating out. Every time I sit down in this kitchen I think your grandmother's right here beside me and it makes me brood. She loved this old house."

"The lady next door said it was for sale."

"Fatso should mind her own business. Mr. Denham, my lawyer friend, is handling the estate but houses are hard to sell nowadays and Amanda had no sense of responsibility at all. Nothing she left was clear. As far as that goes, I get half of anything that's left after the debts are paid."

Mabel began to slide the rings up and down over the blue veins on her bony fingers as if she didn't know what to talk about next.

"You still working for the jewelry firm?" I said.

"Mr. Denham made me quit. I'm getting on in years, Charlie, even if I don't look it, and there comes a time in every woman's life when she needs security and a firm helping hand to fall back on. If everything works out all right, Mr. Denham and I are going to be married the first of the year."

"Those are nice rings," I said. "Are they yours?"

"Why Charlie Flowers, what a thing to say! Your grandmother gave me these rings the week before she died. It was as if she saw the end coming and wanted me to have them, poor soul. She didn't seem to realize it might take me the rest of my life to pay for them." Mabel pulled a handkerchief out of her bosom and put it to her eyes. I had no right to call my grandmother's best friend a thief. On the other hand, she knew what grief could do to a person. In her own case— But I never did find out about her own case because it was time to go to work.

When I got home that night, Maggie and Mrs. O'Reilly were waiting up for me. The old light was back in Mrs. O'Reilly's eyes. "I was just telling Margaret, the first time I saw you I said to myself, now there's a young man who'll be worth a great deal of money some day."

"There doesn't seem to be any money," I said. "Just an old house nobody wants to buy. My grandmother gave her rings to Mabel. Mabel also gets half the house."

"That terrible woman seems to have gotten the lion's share," said Maggie. "I'd hire a lawyer and have him go into this. I wouldn't be surprised if Mabel slipped something into your grandmother's coffee."

"That happens all the time," said Mrs. O'Reilly.

Maggie was going to look up a lawyer on her lunch hour the next day, but it turned out she had a date with Mr. Henderson so she let it slide. When I asked Mr. Barney about it, he shook his head. "Stay away from lawyers,

Charlie. The only lawyer you want to see is the one that's handling the estate."

I took his advice. Mr. Denham had an office on North Avenue but he was never in. Then just when I was thinking of calling the police into the case a letter came addressed to Charles Flowers, Esquire. A junkman had made an offer on my grandmother's personal effects and furniture that would just about pay for the cartage. Mr Denham would be much obliged if I would sign the enclosed release and mail it back as soon as possible. I signed the release and sent it back. The following May another letter came. "Dear Mr. Flowers," it said.

> We have found a buyer for the Cullerton Street property of your late grandmother Mrs. Amanda Slaughter. The purchase price is $2,500 out of which $1,250 is to be paid upon delivery of deed to buyers and they will give a trust deed for the balance of $1,250 payable in monthly installments of $30 until paid. We consider this a very good sale. I am enclosing a deed for you to sign and acknowledge and return it here so we can close the deal. Mrs. Godfrey (Mabel) Denham, my wife, is one half heir to the property left by your late grandmother.

It was signed "Mr. Godfrey Denham, Atty at Law." "You were right," I told Maggie. "Mabel poisoned my grandmother and married the lawyer. What I need now is a lawyer of my own."

"I wouldn't advise it at this stage," said Maggie. "A bird in the hand is worth two in the bush."

So I signed the deed and sent it back to Mr. Denham.

One night in June I came home to find Mrs. O'Reilly

weeping in front of the fireplace. She had just received notice her house was to be sold for taxes. She would have to be out of it in thirty days. Maggie was staring into the empty fireplace, stony-faced, in a new pair of lounging pajamas, waiting for Mrs. O'Reilly to finish her cry so she could hand me a letter that came that morning. It was from Mr. Denham and included a settling of accounts. Half of the $1,250 due me as half-heir was to be paid in monthly installments of $15 each. From the $625 left was subtracted half the balance due on the mortgage, all the funeral expenses, and the money due Mr. Denham for working so hard on the case. There was a check enclosed for the balance—$398.22.

My hands were trembling so hard by the time I got to the end of the letter I could hardly hold the check. Mrs. O'Reilly broke out in tears all over again when I showed it to her. Maggie wouldn't even look at it.

"You know, dove, money's a wonderful thing but unless it comes in large enough quantities, it doesn't mean anything. Will you buy me a drink if I put on some clothes?"

"Yes," I said. "I think my grandmother would like me to do that."

Forty-seventh Street was bright with taverns in those days, each with its red and green neon sign in the window and bowls of popcorn on the bar. Maggie asked if she could order. I said yes and she ordered two whiskey sours. "I drink them all the time," she said, "except when I'm with you."

"You mean you let on you liked ale better because it was all I could afford?"

"That's the long and short of it, darling."

"Those days are gone forever," I said. "Bottoms up!"

After the second whiskey sour, Maggie said, "I'm worried about you. What do you intend to do with that check when you get it cashed?"

"The first thing I'm going to do is pay Mrs. O'Reilly's back taxes."

"Don't you dare. Mrs. O has scads of relatives. Let her live off them for a while. If you get any more bright ideas like that, your check won't last a month. It's not a great deal of money, but at least you can do what you've always wanted to do."

"What's that?"

"Go on with your dancing of course. You can afford lessons now. You may not know it, but I'm going to see that you go through with it. Do you love me?" she said, squeezing my hand under the bar.

"This is a late date to be saying it," I said, "but I always have, I guess, ever since that first time I saw you on the seventh floor at Finley's."

"Go on, darling."

"Go on where?"

"Never mind. May I have another drink?"

"Not unless you tell me what's the matter."

Maggie fiddled with the orange peel hooked over the side of her glass for a few seconds. "You don't have to believe me if you don't want to," she said finally. "I lost my job today."

"But just the other day you said they were going to make you a buyer."

"They were, damn it. I had Henderson on my side, but

the old guard has been putting shoppers on me for months, trying to catch me at something. I pride myself on being able to spot those bitches a mile off but this little mouse took me in completely. She knew exactly what she wanted, no tapered sleeves or padded shoulders, just a simple honest-to-God suit but it had to be a pinstripe. We didn't have a thing like it of course but I remembered seeing just such a suit last Saturday at Belke's on the boulevard. 'But my dear,' I practically gushed, 'I know just the suit you're looking for. I saw it in the window at Belke-Wiel's!' "

"What's Belke-Wiel's?"

"Belke-Wiel's is one of the few shops in the Middle West where you can buy ready-mades that don't look as if they were make-do's."

"What's a make-do?"

"Make-do's are what I've been wearing since Daddy died. It's a word of mine, darling. But I won't bore you with any more details. They hauled me up to the ninth floor so fast for sending a customer to Belke's, it was positively insulting."

"What are you going to do now?"

"I haven't the faintest idea, but I'm tired of selling."

"If you run short of money, will you let me lend you some?"

"You're too damned soft," said Maggie. "You'd make a wonderful touch for a woman without any scruples. Who's going to look out for you after we move?"

"Is moving going to make so much difference?" I said. "I suppose if either of us had any sense we'd hold onto each other. I suppose if we were serious like other people, we'd get married and that would settle everything."

"Would we have to be so goddam serious?"

"You mean you'd even think of marrying me?"

"Why not? Whether you appreciate it or not, I went through hell making up my mind about you. You aren't an easy person to fall in love with."

I couldn't say anything for a minute. All I could do was blow my nose.

"Please don't, darling. I couldn't bear it if you cried."

"I must be getting a cold," I said. "Oh Maggie! Love is the most important thing in the world, isn't it?"

"Next to money, darling."

"Then it's lucky I happen to have some."

"Look here, you don't think I'd marry you for the sake of that lousy little check, do you?"

"No."

"Don't you think it was a funny coincidence that I lost my job today?"

"No. Why?"

Maggie laughed. "Oh darling, you trust people entirely too much. I hate to insult you by saying this but you're so trusting and so pure I wonder how any woman could resist you."

"Most women don't have any trouble," I said.

"That's because you never give them a chance. Do you want to know the real reason I'm marrying you? It's because you say such clever things."

"You and me both," I said. "If we ever have a baby, it should turn out smarter than a trained seal."

"Oh cripes! I knew that would come up. I'm warning you, darling, I hate the little bastards. But I'll marry you—

on one condition—that you give up that awful job at Alexander's."

"I will if you want me to. When do you think we ought to get married?"

"Tomorrow," said Maggie.

There was no waiting to get married in those days. I went downtown the next morning to tell Mr. Barney I was quitting. Maggie went to Finley's to pick up her last paycheck, and we met in the Palmer House and had lunch in the coffee shop. "Look, lamb," said Maggie over dessert. "I despise jewelry so I don't want a ring but I would like a decent dress for a change. Can I buy one at Belke-Wiel's?"

"How much would it cost?"

"God knows, but we'll find out."

I had never been in a store like Belke-Wiel's before. The floors were covered with carpets an inch thick. Maggie insulted a saleslady on the third floor and the saleslady insulted her back. When they had warmed up to each other, Maggie decided a suit would be more practical than a dress and asked to see one like the gray pinstripe in the window. I couldn't picture anyone getting married in June in a suit, even Maggie, but when she tried it on she looked wonderful with her hair falling over the collar like a blond waterfall. The price was $90, not counting the tax. I was still catching my breath when we went to the City Hall for the license.

Maggie took one look at the spittoons in the corridors and said, "Oh darling, if Daddy were alive, he wouldn't want me to be married in this dirty place. Would you mind terribly if we looked up a minister?"

129

"I don't care," I said. "I just want to get it over with."

We found a minister in a church near the Bryson Hotel on the South Side, half a mile from Mrs. O'Reilly's. Maggie's friend Erica had loaned us her Nash for the honeymoon so we went to a subdivision right from the church where there were plenty of paved but empty streets and Maggie taught me to drive. She figured if you wanted to do something you just went ahead and did it. For me it was a brand-new way of looking at things and I won't say I didn't like it.

We wound up at a place in Indiana called Turkey Run, where Maggie had gone with her father once to see the dogwoods coming into bloom. There was a lodge where you could stay. The meals were good and there was a crackling fire in the fireplace after dinner, but the best part about Turkey Run was a small canyon they have there. On our last day we packed a shoebox with sandwiches. Then we checked out of the lodge and followed the canyon to the top of the flat Indiana prairie where it began. After eating the sandwiches, we walked back through the canyon. When we got to the car park I threw the shoebox in the trash can.

"My God!" said Maggie. "Did you ever see anything so ugly and so beautiful at the same time?"

She was staring at a moth on one of the headlamps on the Nash. Its furry yellow body was so big you could almost see its lungs move in and out when it breathed. Its wings were six inches across, pale green, with delicate powdery veins. It was hard to believe moths came that big in Indiana. It might have been blown across the sea from India for all we knew. I touched it with my finger. Its wings trembled but it clung to the headlamp.

"Don't, darling. You'll make me sick."

"If we leave it there, it'll blow off and get run over. Let's get rid of it."

"It might never forgive us. Do you suppose that horrible thing has a soul? Let's put it in the shoebox and take it home."

I fished the shoebox out of the trash can, punched a few holes in the lid, and knocked the thing into the box. Then we headed for Chicago.

Mrs. O'Reilly was waiting up for us. She and Mr. O'Reilly were moving the next day to Benton Harbor where one of her six sisters lived. She had built a fire to use up the last of the magic salts but the fire was out by the time we arrived and she was nodding on a rolled-up rug in front of the fireplace. She didn't really wake up until we took the lid off the shoebox and showed her the moth. It reared up its head and glared. I slapped the lid back on quick and the moth began to thump against the sides of the box. Mrs. O'Reilly got quite alarmed. She wanted to know what we were going to do with it.

"We're going to sell it," said Maggie. "It's worth a great deal of money."

"That reminds me," said Mrs. O'Reilly, feeling nervously in her hair for a pencil that wasn't there. "I sold the double bed yesterday. I hope you don't mind sleeping in Charlie's room tonight."

"Of course I mind," said Maggie. "Suppose you try sleeping in a single bed with Mr. O sometime."

We left Mrs. O'Reilly at the foot of the stairs, trying to make up her mind whether Maggie really minded or not.

It didn't take more than five minutes to discover that

two people would have trouble staying on top of my old bed, let alone sleeping in it, no matter how much in love they were. After an hour of clinging to each other to keep from falling off, we were almost asleep when we heard thumping sounds coming from the shoebox on the dresser.

"Can't you get rid of that damn thing without killing it?" pleaded Maggie.

I slid up the window screen and took the lid off the box but when I tried to dump the moth out, it clung for dear life to the sides of the box. I was afraid of it myself by that time. I pulled the screen down and left the box sitting on the window ledge on the other side of the screen. When we finally did get to sleep it was about as restful as sitting up all night on a three-legged stool. About five o'clock we both woke up with a start. There was a terrible rattling and pounding coming from somewhere.

"It's Junior," I said. "He's beating his brains out against the screen." I got up and tried to drive him away but his little feet clenched the wires of the screen and his wings slammed against it like a wild animal's against the bars of its cage. I lifted the screen and scraped him back into the box and put on the lid. My heart was pounding like a triphammer.

"You're not going to bring that to bed with you!" said Maggie.

"You won't let me kill it. What am I supposed to do? Eat it?"

"I don't care what you do with it," she said. "Just get rid of it. It's your baby."

I took the box in the bathroom and dumped the moth

in the toilet but it flew out and clung panting to the wall. Standing on the rim of the bathtub, I managed to trap it with a towel and shake it out of the towel into the toilet where, half-squashed, its wings still beating against the sides of the bowl, I flushed it down. My hands were spotted with greenish powder like a deadly poison. I washed them, then I went back in the bedroom.

Maggie was standing at the window in her pajamas, staring across the overhead cables of the IC tracks at the yellow strip of sky on the horizon of the lake where the sun was coming up, shivering as if she had a chill.

"I've got to have a drink," she said. "Do you think you could find anything downstairs? I'd settle for a shot of Mr. O's tonic."

"You're crazy," I said. "Get back in bed."

She climbed into bed and I crawled in beside her and put my arms around her. She was trembling like a baby.

"Do you love me, darling? I wouldn't blame you if you didn't."

"This is a hell of a time to be asking that. What do you suppose I married you for?"

"But I didn't really lose my job at Finley's," she said, trembling so hard her teeth began to chatter. "That wasn't true about the shopper. I invented the whole story."

"But I knew that all along."

"Oh Christ, I'll never be able to make it up to you now."

"You already have," I said. "Now go to sleep." And I held her in my arms until sun came up and the trembling died down and she went to sleep.

NINE

After the honeymoon we moved into a furnished apartment
in the Bryson Hotel not far from Mrs. O'Reilly's old house.
The apartment had a kitchen but Maggie preferred to eat
out so we never used it except for mixing drinks. Each night
after dinner I would fix her a highball and she would curl
up with a detective story under the floor lamp. Maggie had
a mind like an electric clock. It didn't tick. It gave off just
enough of a whirr so you knew it was operating. One night
she closed her book and said, "Have you ever noticed
Belke's windows, darling—Belke-Wiel's on the boulevard,
where I bought my suit?"

"They were full of brooms the last time I saw them."

"And chicken wire draped with summer prints. Belke's have the most imaginative window displays in Chicago. Have you ever noticed how many people stop to look at Belke's display and how few bother to look at Bandello's? That's the shoe store next door. Their windows are sordid by comparison."

"When you look in a shoe store you expect to see shoes, not brooms."

"You're very amusing," said Maggie, "but I'm not in the mood tonight. Sitting around day after day is driving me crazy. We've been married four weeks today but you haven't done a thing about your dancing that I can see."

"Suppose I did take lessons. Where would I practice? What would the management at the Bryson say when I started digging up the tile in their bathroom with the taps of my shoes? Anyway it's too hot. I think I'll wait until October. There's enough money left to last a couple of months. After that I'll still be getting payments from my grandmother's house."

"Considering we're paying fifty-five dollars for an apartment," said Maggie, "fifteen dollars a month isn't a great deal of money. But it's only a fraction of what you'll make when you get that personality of yours ironed out and offered for sale, my love. Do you know what I think I'll do tomorrow? Go down to Bandello's and offer to renovate their windows for them. And I don't want any silly twaddle about the man being the mainstay of the family. You will be, eventually, and I'll welcome that day, but in the interval I don't intend to pine away in a quaint rooming house. Or in a crumby hotel for that matter."

"You never decorated a window in your life," I said. "They'll laugh at you. They'll turn you down."

"They won't turn me down. You should know by now, darling, when I get an idea I act on it and the devil take the hindmost. If Mr. Bandello offers me less than fifty a week he's going to feel very embarrassed."

Maggie went downtown the next morning. When she came home at six o'clock I kissed her and she said, "If there's liquor on my breath, it comes from the Blackhawk and I don't mean the poolroom either. My new boss bought me a drink."

"Mr. Bandello?"

"There is no such person, darling. I was prepared to be aloof in case Mr. Bandello turned out to be Latin and passionate. What was my surprise to find that Bandello's is owned by a couple of smart Jews named Herskowitz. Fix me a bourbon with a drop of gingerale in it. I'll tell you all about it."

Maggie had started off by buying a pair of shoes. "I pretended I was a buyer from Finley's. That brought the younger Herskowitz running. I told him I was making a study of merchandising methods so he took me up to his office for what he thought was a free advertising consultation. Darling, you'd never believe it but the brothers Herskowitz have been doing the windows themselves. I told them quite frankly what I thought of their displays. They wanted to argue all morning. I insisted I had to be back at Finley's but I promised to meet them for a drink at four. So I had lunch with Erica and went shopping until it was time to pick up the lonely Herskowitz brother. That's the one that's separated from his wife."

"Did he offer you a job?"

"A bed was what he had in mind. However, I offered to work for him if they'd let me revitalize their displays. It's thirty a week to start, but I can buy any amount of shoes at a discount."

"You said you wouldn't take less than fifty."

"But darling," said Maggie, looking hurt, "there are times when you simply have to compromise."

It didn't take Maggie long to find out she was at sea in a shoe store. When she came home at night I would fix her a drink and she would complain about how terrible the August windows turned out to be. They were so full of shoes she could hardly see the cardboard skyscrapers in the background.

"Oh darling," she complained, "do you suppose I'm a failure as a window decorator? The September windows will really have to be knockouts or it will all be over between me and Bandello's. We've got some lovely slippers in, all heels. I want lots of fences in the window and autumn leaves. I'd like to get hold of a dress to drape over the fence that will stop traffic. The only thing I can't figure out is what to do with the shoes."

"You could hang them on brooms," I suggested.

"That's unkind, darling, but it gives me an idea. I have half a mind to go next door to Belke's tomorrow and see if they'll let me have a dress. A formal with brilliant peppermint stripes would do."

When Maggie suggested borrowing a dress for the window, the Herskowitz brothers just laughed. That didn't stop Maggie from barging into Belke's and telling them she wanted to borrow their most startling evening gown for a window full of shoes. The manager took her to the advertising manager who took her to the private office of Mr. Belke himself. "Would you believe it," said Maggie when she got home that night, "Mr. Belke didn't think my idea was crazy at all. He just thought that if Bandello's wanted a dress that badly they should pay for it. But the important thing is that Hubert Belke recognized me. He was a senior at Chicago during my freshman year."

"Let me guess what happens next," I said. "Mr. Wiel steps out from behind a curtain and pinches your behind."

"Don't be vulgar. Wiel is old lady Belke's maiden name. She practically ran the Michigan Avenue shop single-handed while Hubert was going to school. The curious thing is that I don't remember him at all. I pretended to of course. He took me out afterwards and bought me a drink."

"They all do," I said.

"Darling, I think you're jealous. If you could see this Belke person you wouldn't be. You're really quite a man by comparison. But he has wonderful taste. We didn't drink just anything. We had Cointreau, the kind with the clown on the bottle, fifty-five cents the thimbleful."

"I can remember when we used to drink beer."

"That was before we were rich," said Maggie, stopping to light a cigarette. "Now for the exciting part. Mr. Belke wants me to work for him. He wants me to sell so naturally I turned him down. But I can't hold out much longer against the brothers Herskowitz. They had the nerve to suggest at lunch yesterday that I buy the drinks for a change. I'm beginning to think they're nothing but a couple of cheap kikes."

"I thought you were so broad-minded about the Jews."

"But nobody is more broad-minded than I," said Maggie. "All the same it would be nice to work for a person like Hubert Belke for a change. I've got until Friday to make up my mind. He wants me to drop around on Friday and meet Jolly. Jolly's a lawyer who designs Belke's windows as a hobby. He doesn't have to practice very hard. I gather from what Hubert says that he has an independent income. I don't imagine this Jolly person is much less effeminate than our little friend Belke," said Maggie, sitting down on the arm of my chair. "Men like that fascinate me. We had some interesting discussions on abnormal psychology when I took psychology at the university. Am I boring you by any chance?"

"If anything's boring me, it's a tapeworm," I said. "Let's have dinner at Chloe's and then go in a bar on 47th Street and drink nothing but beer, just like old times."

"What a marvelous idea," said Maggie, so we did but it was not like old times.

A week later Maggie went to work at Belke-Wiel's, selling dresses for forty dollars a week. "It was Jolly who talked me into it," she explained. "As Hubert says, if I'm thinking of breaking into the business, I'd best learn from the bottom up. I've already given him a couple of good ideas, such as a low-priced line to be merchandised under another label. I honestly think something should be done for the average American woman who can't afford to put more than forty-five dollars into a suit. It was a chance remark that brought the subject up in the first place. I was telling Jolly last Friday how tired I was of make-do's. 'Make-do's?' said Jolly. 'What's a make-do?' "

"I asked you that once."

"Did you, doll? Well, the effect was positively electric. Jolly said, 'How about a make-do line, Hubert? Maggie's little make-do's.' They think it's a wonderful word. It seems I've been using it all these years without realizing that it had any commercial value. The difficulty seems to lie with the old lady, Hubert's mother. She's set in her ways naturally and refuses to think about clothes quantity-produced. But Hubert thinks I have wonderful ideas. I've already given Jolly a ducky idea for his November window. Jolly decorates interiors as well as windows. He once helped do a basement barroom in a North Side hotel for the brother of his law partner, a man by the name of Brogsitter. By the way, darling, I've already told Hubert and Jolly you're a professional dancer. They want to meet you soon."

"Why should they want to meet me?"

"Because I'm married to you, damn it, even if I do use my maiden name. I might say Jolly seems almost indecently interested in meeting you," she added with a smile. "Hubert wants us to come up to his apartment on Lake Shore Drive some evening to meet the old lady. He has a sister too. She lives on the South Side not far from here. Her name's Belle."

"I don't want to meet any rich people," I said.

"You don't seem to have much else to do," said Maggie. "When are you going to do something about your dancing?"

"You won't believe me but I went downtown yesterday. Mr. Barney sent me to this former pupil of his who teaches. But he wants too much. Anyway, I can just see that old buzzard at the desk downstairs when he discovers I've been scratching up the floors in the Bryson."

"Don't let that worry you. It's time we were moving out of this hole. I'm having lunch with Belle Belke tomorrow. She might have an idea."

"Oh for God sake," I said, "why do we always have to be talking about the Belkes?"

But we always were talking about them and not long after that, it seemed, they moved into our life and took over.

TEN

The old Belke house was on a corner in an exclusive neighborhood not far from the Bryson Hotel, a regular little island of old families and Chicago refinement. Years ago the stable in back had been converted into a garage and the harness room upstairs had been turned into an apartment for the chauffeur. When old man Belke died, Mrs. Belke and Hubert moved into an apartment on Lake Shore Drive. The chauffeur was fired along with the cook. Belle Belke had stayed on in the old-fashioned red brick house, living alone with a maid named Lily, a houseman named John, and a Saint Bernard by the name of Tiny.

Belle Belke was a father's girl like Maggie so they got along well. The second time they had lunch together Maggie suggested Belle should rent us the vacant apartment above her garage, and the following Sunday we walked over to have a look at it. Tiny followed us up the narrow stairs of the old stable, sweeping away the cobwebs with his tail. The bathroom was so small he couldn't turn around. Miss Belke had to back him out of it.

"It doesn't look like much of an apartment," I said.

"It's a garage apartment, darling. They're very desirable right now."

"But we don't have any furniture."

"Furniture!" screamed Miss Belke. "My God, man, there's an attic full of it going to rack and ruin. You can have your pick. As for the decorating, Jolly's been after me for years to have the place done over."

"Don't you see," said Maggie as we walked back to the Bryson, "it's an ideal setup. You can practice dancing to your heart's content in the garage downstairs. I haven't the faintest idea what it will cost to furnish the dump, but I'm making forty-five a week now and Hubert's promised to take me off selling and give me a substantial raise if he can get his mother to agree to the make-do line."

"Did Miss Belke say what the rent would be?"

"Darling," said Maggie, "there are some things you don't discuss with the Belkes and money is one of them."

Surprisingly enough, the rent turned out to be only fifteen dollars a month so as soon as the toilet was fixed we moved in. Miss Belke went over the furniture in the attic of the big house and pointed out the pieces we could take and those we couldn't. With everything else she gave Maggie a free hand. Maggie began by asking Lily for half a dozen sheets the first day, a few bath towels the next. Then it was china, then silver and glassware. When I asked why we couldn't live more simply, she said, "Beggars can't be choosers. At least we have a roof over our heads. And liquor in the house. That's important too when it comes to weathering the depression. We won't always be poor."

"For poor people we seem to be doing OK," I said. "If you look a little deeper you'll find a flaw in the ointment somewhere. What's the decorating going to cost?"

"It's going to cost plenty to bring this stable up to my standards," said Maggie, "but I don't intend to pay for it myself."

For a long time, the only decorating that was done consisted of long arguments between Maggie and Jolly in downtown bars over what color to have the bathroom. Maggie had the idea Jolly would pay for everything if she let him pick the colors. When he didn't offer to pay for anything she decided to pay for it herself, then at the last minute Jolly broke down and offered to reupholster the old-fashioned Belke sofa and chairs. They came back two weeks later all done up in red and green and yellow stripes.

"You mean Jolly did all that by himself?" I said.

"He selected the materials, darling."

"Well, if he doesn't stuff furniture or paint ceilings or hang wallpaper, how can he call himself a decorator?"

"Don't be naive," said Maggie. "He has exquisite taste."

While the decorating was going on I was discovering my feet again. Mr. Barney dug up a teacher for me, a middle-aged Puerto Rican with an absent-minded way of snapping his pants legs five or six inches above his ankles to show his small feet to better advantage when he demonstrated a break. He had a studio in the Auditorium Building behind the old opera house. Sometimes in that little room with a hot piano going full blast, the old juices seemed to leak back into my feet but in the cold garage next to Miss Belke's big Buick they seemed to leak out again. Nobody could figure out who was paying for the lessons. We drifted along on the idea that whatever Maggie gave me on payday was in payment for the inheritance we spent so lavishly during our three months at the Bryson. "It's your money as well as mine," she said. "It's just until you get started."

"But I never will get started. It takes years of experience and even then you never get anywhere without a break. Who'd give me a break?"

"That's my department, darling. When it comes to that, I may have a little surprise for you soon. In the meantime you stick to your dancing. And the cooking. That's your department."

One afternoon Maggie came home early and caught me practicing. That night after dinner she said, "That business you were doing this afternoon looked tremendously complicated. You must be very good by now."

"I'm not," I said. "It makes me feel like a pet monkey to have someone watching like that."

"Don't be ridiculous. What you need is an audience. An intimate little club would be just the ticket. Let the dishes go for a few minutes. I have some news for you, darling. Jolly's law partner, Brogsitter, has found a spot on the Near North Side where he's willing to open a small exclusive club if Hubert will put up the money. This is Jolly's chance to do another club. It's your chance too, dove. I wouldn't be at all surprised if Mr. Brogsitter manages to find a place for you in the floor show."

So that was Maggie's surprise. As far as I was concerned it was just another crazy idea of hers like finding an apartment above a garage because I needed a place to practice. Maggie didn't know much about people who used their feet to make a living instead of their heads. She didn't know much about nightclubs either. They had mushroomed all over the place with the return of liquor but it was easier to squeeze a singer and an accordian onto a floor the size of a napkin than a dancer. It was no secret that half the ushers in the downtown movie houses were ex-hoofers, waiting for breaks that never came.

"It won't work," I said.

"Of course it will. Jolly thinks it's a marvelous idea. I've already told him how you used to sit among the cobwebs in your grandmother's attic and watch Al Jolson when he was a singing waiter at the Melody Gardens and Fred Astaire when he was a mere stripling."

"That's a lie. The Melody Gardens were never big time, even in those days."

"Don't get riled, pet. Jolly loves touches like that. Fix me a drink. I'll take mine straight if we don't have any soda. Jolly made me swear off ginger ale last night. It's much too sissified. Nothing but bonded bourbon and soda from now on. Where did we get this rotgut?"

"On 47th Street when we were still poor," I said, handing her a shot of whiskey in one of Miss Belke's best

146

tumblers. "Last night was the second time this week you had dinner downtown."

"It's not my fault I have to eat with Jolly alone. I'm getting damned tired of making excuses for you all the time."

"Nobody ever invited me," I said in surprise. "Do you want me to go out with you?"

"Not if you feel the way you do about my friends. And while we're on the subject, why don't you have any friends of your own? Other men do."

I was sitting next to Maggie on the sofa and just naturally slipped my hand inside her dress and began fooling around. "I can't feel for your friends like I feel for you," I said.

"Darling, sit up! Sometimes you're positively distressing. And don't change the subject. You could have lots of friends. Hubert's jealous of you because you're married to me, but Jolly's perfectly willing to be your friend."

"I thought you meant men friends."

"Now doll, you're not such a he-man you can afford to talk like that about Hubert and Jolly. That was a rather vulgar remark. I hope you won't be quite so vulgar in front of the Belkes. Funny, yes, but not vulgar."

"Oh for God sake," I said. "When do I ever get a chance to be vulgar in front of the Belkes?"

"Haven't I told you? We're invited to Mrs. Belke's for dinner on Friday. The old lady almost never comes down to the store anymore on account of her neuralgia, but I wangled a dinner invitation from Hubert. His mother's terribly curious about you. She practically refuses to believe

I'm married. There's only one thing, darling. I've told the old lady you had an income so don't make any breaks."

"Why did you have to lie about it?"

"It's not a lie. You get a check from your grandmother's estate every month."

"Fifteen dollars!"

"Well," said Maggie, "that's an income of sorts."

There was a roaring fire in the fireplace of the big Belke apartment on Lake Shore Drive Friday night that put Mrs. O'Reilly's magic salts to shame. A portrait of old man Belke was built into the paneling above the fireplace. Hubert Belke didn't look anything like his father. There was a plumpness about him like an overripe melon but you sensed there was a solid businessman underneath. He smelled of soap. His mother was not bad to look at but her cheek twitched. In addition, she was slightly deaf so everyone had to shout at her to keep up the myth that her ears operated OK.

During dinner a conversation about President Roosevelt raged around the table. I didn't pay much attention until Jolly said in his high husky voice, "Don't tell me Charlie's for Rosenfelt too." Suddenly everyone was looking at me.

"What?"

"But darling, don't be such a mouse," said Maggie. "What's your opinion of the man?"

There was a moment of silence while I tried to think of something to say. "I don't know," I said and took a drink of water.

After dinner everyone went in the living room. Hubert and Jolly were going to show us pictures of their trip to

France. While they tinkered with the movie projector, Maggie found a record player with some classical record albums in it. She put three records on the changer and curled up in front of the loudspeaker with a cigarette, leaving me alone with Mrs. Belke.

"Come closer, Mr. Werner," said the old lady in a voice as full of ripples as her silver hair. "I hear you're very clever."

"My name is Flowers."

"What?"

"Yes," I said "I am."

"What do you do?"

"I don't do anything."

"Maggie says you have an income."

"I inherited some money from my grandmother."

"What?"

"I said I inherited a lot of money."

"How much?"

"I don't know," I shouted. "I never counted it."

Maggie got alarmed at all the shouting and came over. "What are you two lovebirds cooing about?" she said.

"I was about to tell Mr. Werner how very sweet you were to me the first time I saw you at the store. You thought I was a customer, didn't you, Maggie?"

"Indeed not. Hubert had told me all about you. I knew exactly who you were and was anxious to make a good impression."

Mrs. Belke chuckled. She chuckled so hard her cheek was taken with a fit of twitching and everyone had to stand around until the twitching died down.

"What a beautiful shawl," said Maggie to fill in the silence.

"I picked it up in Switzerland last year," said the old lady with a twitch.

"Jolly, look! What an exciting red. How about duplicating it in the stripes around our bar?

"Now, now. Let's not get Jolly started on the windows tonight."

"This is definitely not a discussion about windows," shouted Maggie. "I was thinking of the club."

"Club?"

"The nightclub. Haven't the boys told you?"

"It's nothing, dear," shouted Hubert. "Shall we have the movies?"

"How can a nightclub be nothing?"

"Oh lord!" said Jolly in his normal voice so the old lady wouldn't hear. "You've done it now."

"I hadn't realized it before," said Maggie when we got home that night, "but you're something of a social blank. I keep telling my friends you're the cleverest person I know and they wait for you to say something with their tongues hanging out, so to speak, but the only time you open your mouth all you have to say is 'I don't know.' You never clammed up like that at the O'Reilly's."

"That was different. The O'Reillys were poor like us, not rich like the Belkes."

"Don't be stupid. The Belkes have made their pile. We're still on the make. That's the only difference."

"I don't get it," I said. "Was this whole thing your

idea? Because if it is, it's time you came to your senses. It won't work. I'm not worth it."

"Of course you are or I wouldn't have married you. This time you're not going to throw your chances away. You're going to make a go of it. I'll divorce you if you don't."

"Go ahead. See if I care. Anyway if you're so clever why did you get so embarrassed when the old lady asked about the club? Wasn't she supposed to know?"

"No, damn it. When Jolly turned on me like that I was as shocked as if he'd slapped me in the face."

"It wouldn't be her money, would it?"

"It would be Hubert's and that amounts to the same thing. Oh darling, I'm so ashamed. I coached you so carefully, yet I made the crudest break of all. Now the old lady may veto the whole idea and I was counting on you to charm the old bitch. Did you manage to say something clever?"

"She didn't give me the chance. All she wanted to talk about was money. Money isn't that important."

"It is when you don't have it," said Maggie.

Maggie wasn't the type to let anyone stand in her way, not even Mrs. Belke, but toward the end of May she came to her senses with a jolt when she discovered she was pregnant.

ELEVEN

It was a warm May night. The kitchen window was open and the smell of lilacs drifted into the apartment above the garage. It was so still for a few seconds you could hear Tiny stirring in his sleep on the back porch of the Belkes' big house.

"Did you hear me?" said Maggie. "I said I'm pregnant."

"I heard you," I said. "Just because I don't jump up and down like I was shot doesn't mean I haven't any sails to take the wind out of. I'm dumbfounded, that's all." I took

Maggie in my arms and kissed her on the neck. "Can't you just picture it," I said, "the patter of little feet, the dripping of little pants?"

"No, I can't picture it. Unfortunately I'm the one that's going to have the baby, not you. I'm going to get rid of it if I possibly can."

"You mean you're going to kill it?"

"Darling! You frighten me sometimes. I mean there are things to take. There are people to see."

Maggie took some tablets over the weekend and sat around all Sunday in knots from the pain. That didn't do any good so she went to see a doctor Erica recommended. She came home looking gray. "He says he can fix me up but I don't trust him," she said. "I think I'll ask Jolly. He might know a better doctor."

One of Jolly's friends was a doctor it turned out. Maggie had her own name for him—Baggypants. "His fees are horribly high and his pants are never pressed but he seems to know his business," she said. "He says the only safe thing to do is have the baby. Oh darling, let's be more careful in the future. This is going to cost a heap of money. I'll need new clothes. Nothing will fit."

"I'd better go down to Alexander's and get my old job back."

"Don't you dare. I need you at home. The money doesn't bother me half as much as my job. I'd hate to have anything happen to it. I'll have to take a couple of months off as it is."

I did everything I could to help, keeping the house clean, fixing Maggie breakfasts that would stay down, thinking up menus that would snag her appetite when she came home from work at night. After September she only had to work four hours a day but she got paid for a full day. Every other day she would come home with a new maternity outfit.

"Don't be alarmed, darling. It didn't cost a cent. Hubert calls me his human guinea pig. He's been letting me shop. I had the pleasure of shopping Finley's today. This material is first-rate but the design is something awful. You'd think motherhood was a crime the way they muffle you up in drab colors and pleats to be let out. Hubert thinks I've made a valuable psychological discovery. Bright colors can do more to detract attention from the bulge than all the navy-blue pleats in Lane-Bryant's. It's better for the mother's psychology too. I've been doing some high-powered talking down at the store. I've even been out to see the old lady a couple of times and you know how conservative she is. Belke-Wiel's is going to do something about the situation. But soon, darling."

One day toward the end of October when Maggie was really beginning to bulge, she came home and said, "Hubert hinted he has a little surprise for me tomorrow morning when I open the *Tribune*. He wouldn't let me see the proofs but don't be shocked if you see a maternity frock in Belke's ad tomorrow with *Maggie Werner Original* somewhere on the page in large type." When Maggie came home the following afternoon she slammed the morning paper on the kitchen table where I was cutting up some expensive California strawberries for her lunch and said, "Rats! Look at this."

It was a quarter-page ad announcing the expanded maternity department at Belke-Wiel's. In the middle was a sketch of a woman leading a greyhound on a leash. The dog had no stomach at all. If the woman had one, her jacket stuck out so far you couldn't see it. Underneath the picture it said A MATERNITY MAKE-DO, ONLY AT BELKE-WIEL'S.

"What's a maternity make-do?"

"It's what I'm wearing but that's not the point. Hubert practically promised to use my name when we brought out the new line."

"That's your word, isn't it, make-do? Maybe that's what he meant."

"You're very reassuring in your simple way, dove. In the long run I'll get the credit I deserve, but the next time Hubert hints he has a surprise for me I wish he wouldn't be so goddam coy."

Maggie wasn't really displeased. Jolly arranged a window of maternity make-do's. The models had safety pins for eyes, and their stomachs stuck out so far in all directions they stopped traffic on Michigan Boulevard. Maggie began to feel she had established herself at Belke-Wiel's almost as solid as if she had married Hubert Belke instead of me.

She quit work the first of December. She was so sure the baby would arrive early she had Baggypants make arrangements at the hospital on Stony Island Avenue a month in advance. We were invited to the big house for dinner Christmas Eve but Mrs. Belke was going to be there and Maggie didn't want the old lady to see her in her condition. She insisted the doctor wouldn't let her leave the garage, so Hubert and Jolly and Belle came out in the backyard and sang Christmas carols while Maggie sat at the window in her red corduroy make-do and pretended to be thrilled. Afterwards Lily brought up a silver tray loaded with Tom and Jerries.

When Maggie was on her second Tom and Jerry she grabbed my hand and pressed it to her stomach. "My God, darling, just feel!" It was hard to tell if the two lumps were a baby's knees or its behind. Whatever they were, they were sure moving around. "I wish it was over," she said. "It frightens the hell out of me. I don't know if you realize it or not, but I'm a terrible sissy when it comes to pain. Daddy didn't die an easy death. He lasted three days and I was with him every minute. He just lay there and took it but I'm not that type. When I'm hurt, I scream, and I'll do a lot of screaming before this is over. I won't blame you if you turn tail and run. I'll frighten you out of your wits."

"The only time you frighten me is when you suggest I won't stand by you," I said.

"Thanks, doll. For once you've said the right thing. I couldn't bear to go through this with anyone else. Do you love me?"

"Twice as much," I said.

"Then stand by me, darling. Please."

Belle Belke went to Lake Geneva the first of the year for a few weeks, leaving instructions with Lily to bring over Maggie's dinner each night. I hadn't had a haircut for five weeks but whenever I offered to get one, Maggie said, "No, darling. I'm sure it's going to come today. I couldn't bear to be alone when it started."

The Saturday after New Year's Maggie let me go down to 47th Street to pick up a few groceries. When I got home she had her coat on. She looked scared.

"It's started, darling. Phone Baggypants and order a cab."

Lily was very calm. "Don't bother with a cab," she said. "John will drive you to the hospital." The doctor didn't sound any more excited than Lily. "How far apart are the pains?" he said.

"Are they supposed to be apart? I'll see," I said and ran back to the garage.

"How the hell should I know?" said Maggie. "If Baggypants thinks I'm going to sit around the house with a stopwatch, he's mistaken. Tell him I'm on my way to the hospital."

Miss Belke's houseman had the Buick warmed up and out of the garage by the time I got through talking to the doctor. We climbed in back and Maggie squeezed my hand.

"They're quite regular now."

"Does it hurt?"

"You'll know when it hurts, darling. I'll scream."

They had a nice waiting room for fathers in that hospital. I sat in it for four hours and watched the snow falling into the trees in Jackson Park across the way. I figured Maggie would be doubled up with pain when they finally let me see her, but she was sitting up in bed, smoking a cigarette and looking at the pictures in a fashion magazine. "They've been doing the most awful things to me," she complained. "First they shaved me like a burlesque queen, then they gave me an enema. The pains stopped as soon as I got into bed and now the head nurse refuses to send for Baggypants. If they haven't started again by morning, they're going to send me home."

"They can't do that."

"Don't worry, darling. I'm not budging from this hospital until it's over."

I went home and went to bed. Early Sunday I called the hospital from the big house and they let me speak to Maggie. She sounded so normal you could picture her sitting on the nurse's desk in the corridor in her housecoat, flicking ashes on the floor under the No Smoking sign. "Hello, doll," she said. "I've got Baggypants on the job. If nothing's happened by noon, he's going to give me something to induce labor."

I went back to the hospital that afternoon and sat in the waiting room with another father until his doctor came in and announced a seven-pound girl and he went away to look at it. At six o'clock Maggie's doctor showed up. "We've tried to induce labor but it's not going well," he said. "I'd advise you to go home."

He arranged for me to see Maggie before he left. A nurse wheeled her out of the labor room into the hallway. Her stomach bulged under the sheet. Her face was like wax. "I've had pains all afternoon but Baggypants won't give me the dope because he's not sure they're real labor pains. Here comes one now," she said, grasping my hand. "Oh! That was a good one, darling. No, don't call the nurse. The nurses are disgusted with me. I can't get any service out of them at all. Will you give me a cigarette?" I lit one for her. She got two good puffs out of it before a nurse came by and made me put it out.

For the second time in two days I went home to an empty house. The sound of a cab coming to a stop outside the garage woke me up Monday morning. A minute later Maggie toddled up the garage steps and flopped on the sofa.

"What happened?"

"Nothing, damn it. I spent the night in the labor room. Two women groaned and screamed all night long. This morning I was falling into the most beautiful sleep when the head nurse sent me back to my room. She's been gunning for me for two days now. She wouldn't even let me talk to Baggypants when he called. He told her to send me home. So here I am." She belched and clutched her side. "Don't look at me like that. I'm not going to blow up. Why don't you stop acting like a prospective father and go out and get your hair cut?"

"You might have the baby while I'm gone."

"If I'm going to sit around the house for another week looking at that awful mop of yours, I never will have it. Tell Lily you're going so she can look in on me."

Haircuts were cheap in those days. You paid fifty cents and got a dollar's worth of conversation in return. It took a long time. I hurried home as fast as I could. As I rounded the corner I could hear Lily calling John from the window of the garage. I ran up the stairs three at a time. Maggie was stretched out on the sofa in the red maternity make-do from Belke-Wiel's, groaning and biting on a washrag.

"She lost the water, Mr. Flowers," said Lily.

Maggie took the washrag out of her mouth.

"Never mind that. Do something, darling."

"John's getting the car out," said Lily. "There's nothing to do."

"I can't ride in a car," wailed Maggie. "Get Baggypants. Hurry. For God's sake!"

I brushed past John who was putting on his coat in the kitchen of the big house and picked up the telephone. "All right," said the doctor. "Get her to the hospital. I'll be there as soon as I can."

When I got back to the garage, Lily was putting pans of water on the stove. There was a satisfied smile on her face.

"Did you get the doctor?" said Maggie from the sofa.

"Yes. He's on his way to the hospital."

"You goddam fool, I can't make the hospital. Tell him to come here."

I ran back to the house, my legs buckling at every step. A nurse answered the phone. The doctor had just left for the hospital, could she take a message? No I said and hung up. Then I didn't know what to do. Suddenly my eyes focused on the cover of the telephone directory where it said, "In case of emergency call—"

"Police thirteen-thirteen," I told the operator, reading the number off the book. A policeman answered. When I told him my wife was having a baby he said, "It happens every day, Jack. Why don't you take her to the hospital?" When I tried to explain he cut me short. "What's the address? Isn't that the Belke place?" he said when I told him. "Now don't you worry, Mr. Belke. You just relax. We'll take care of everything."

The sirens began to wail before I even got back to the garage. That quiet street, always empty at that time of day, was suddenly full of people and cars. Three policemen and an ambulance driver with a stretcher over his shoulder ran up the steps of the big house. John set them straight and they came running back to the garage. Tiny thundered up the steps at their heels, barking and booming until the policemen chased him out.

It was a beautiful ambulance. If it hadn't been for the sirens on the motorcycles and the squad car you wouldn't have known you were moving. When they slid the stretcher out in front of the hospital the blanket caught on the ambulance steps, exposing Maggie's red corduroy make-do. Her head rolled from side to side but she didn't scream.

Twenty minutes later the doctor walked in the waiting

room. "It's a boy," he said. "Five pounds, six ounces. Mrs. Flowers is doing nicely. There was just time for a whiff of ether at the end. Has there ever been any foot trouble in the family, Mr. Flowers?" he said. "Deformity of any kind?"

My heart gave a thump. "Why?" I said.

"The ankles aren't perfect. It's an easy condition to correct but I'd like your permission to call in a bone specialist."

"Sure, get a specialist," I said. "Will that cost extra?"

"I'm afraid so," said the doctor. "Your wife will be out of the ether in fifteen or twenty minutes. Why don't you get a cup of coffee while you're waiting?"

"I'll wait here," I said. Finally a nurse came in and said, "You can see Mrs. Flowers for a few minutes now." While we were walking down the hall, she said, "When your wife is more coherent, you might explain to her that we'll have another private room for her this afternoon. The room she had this morning was occupied just after she left."

Maggie was flat as a pancake. She didn't open her eyes until I bent down and kissed her.

"That's ether on my breath," she said. "Ought to try it sometime, darlin'. Gives you the most wonderful jag. What were all those bells and whistles?"

"Those were sirens. We had a motorcycle escort. They thought we were Belkes."

"But darlin', what a stroke of genius! Belle will die when I tell her."

Maggie refused to believe it had been an accident. She began to giggle but it hurt her side so she kissed my hand and laid it against her cheek. Then she caught sight of the other women in the room and said in a drunken whisper,

"This isn't my room. This is a ward. Who are all these ugly frumps?" Before I could explain she closed her eyes and went back to sleep.

The woman in the next bed smiled. "You mustn't feel ashamed," she said. "We all say things we don't mean to say when we're coming out of it. It was a boy, wasn't it? Have you seen him yet?"

"Would they let me?"

"Of course they would. The nursery is at the end of the corridor."

A nurse came to the door of the nursery. I gave her my name and she wheeled a metal basket over to the window with a baby in it. It was as wrinkled as a monkey. Its feet were long and the ankles stuck out on the inside as if they had been screwed on the wrong way. The only pretty thing about it was the bracelet on one of its wrists, blue beads alternating with tiny white blocks with letters on them that spelled out the name F-L-O-W-E-R-S.

The nurse smiled. "That's such a lovely name. What's his first name?" "I don't know," I said. Then I said, "Joe I guess." That was the first name that popped into my head. Evidently I didn't sound much like a father. The nurse stopped smiling and cocked her head to one side.

"You are Mr. Flowers, aren't you?"

"Who did you think I was," I said, "the King of Siam?"

TWELVE

"When I woke up in that horrible ward I was high as a kite on ether," said Maggie. "Can you imagine, darling, me in a ward with three other women? When they moved me out of that place, the witch in the next bed was nursing her baby. The noise made me positively ill. Now there are these ugly things to worry about. Baggypants is giving me epsom salts to dry me up."

"You mean you're not going to nurse him?" I said.

"But darling, nobody nurses a baby any more. Have you seen the wizened little monkey yet? He looks like you did before you got your hair cut. I wouldn't be surprised if he had fleas."

"He just looks hungry to me."

"You're a hopeless sentimentalist. You know that, don't you?"

"I don't care about him one way or the other," I said. "I'm just interested in getting him patched up."

"Patched up! Is this something I'm not supposed to know? I hate it when people keep things from me. You might as well tell me, darling."

"Well, the doctor had a specialist in yesterday to look at the baby's feet. The ankles turn in for some reason. They're going to put him in casts for a few weeks. Only they have to wait until his bones grow a little."

"Oh Christ, I might have known I'd give birth to a monstrosity. A specialist will cost money. Look here. Have you thought of a name?"

"Joe."

"Don't be so conventional. How about Hubert? Naming him after a Belke ought to be good for the hospital bill."

"You can't mean it," I said.

"Of course I mean it. You leave the name to me, darling. Now run along and look at the little angel. I'm expecting company."

When I got home that afternoon there was a paperhanger in the bedroom. He was putting up new baby-blue wallpaper covered with silver stars. Jolly paid for it. Belle had a baby buggy sent out from Finley and Dunlap's, the biggest damn buggy she could find, with the thickest tires and the highest springs, as if she had Tiny in mind when she picked it out. Hubert's gift arrived the morning Maggie came home from the hospital. It was the first thing she saw when she got in the house—a large box wrapped in silver paper, tied with a big blue bow. There was a white card on top of the box: "To Little Hubert from Big Hubert." While Maggie was opening the package I laid the baby in the crib in the bedroom.

"Hurry, darling," shouted Maggie from the living room. "You'll never guess what's in the package."

It was a case of Scotch.

"Now aren't you glad we called him Hubert? We didn't name him after a Belke for nothing."

"I hate Scotch," I said. "I get revolted just smelling it."

"But it's lovely with soda. Will you fix me a drink?"

I fixed us each a stiff one. When I came out of the kitchen Maggie was stretched out on the striped sofa with her shoes off. "God, but this is expensive stuff," she said. "Want to know something, darling? I'm getting my ankles back. It would have been very humiliating if they'd just dissolved in a mass of fat. Oh Christ!" she said as the baby began to yap in the bedroom. "There it blows. He can't even wait until we finish our first drink. Run along and ask him what he wants."

Maggie brought a strict feeding schedule home from the hospital with her. When the baby woke up at one A.M. instead of two, she pulled the covers over her head. "Madam," I said, "your baby is crying."

"Then feed him for God's sake. You know how."

After that I fed him whenever he cried. He would stop yapping as soon as the nipple hit his gums and bang away at the bottle until an ounce or two was gone, then he was off to dreamland again. Later, when his eyes began to focus, he would stay awake while he ate and his eyes would jerk from star to star in the blue wallpaper as if he was trying to figure out where he was and what he was doing there. It was strange to think that I could feel so tender toward a baby but I did. I began to look forward to the day when I could make the formula and change his pants without first having to empty ashtrays or fix Maggie a Scotch and soda. Then one day the doctor told Maggie it would be OK to go up and down stairs so she went downtown and did some shopping and the next morning she went back to work at Belke-Wiel's.

When the baby was seven weeks old we took him downtown to the bone specialist to have his ankles put in casts. The specialist slapped on the plaster in long wet ribbons like bandages. He said two or three weeks in casts ought to do the trick. As he talked, the ribbons climbed higher and higher until the only thing left of the baby below the crotch were his toes peeping out of the casts like the kernels of corn on the small end of a cob. There had always been a pleasant smell to him, a mixture of growing hair and milky breath, now there was a new smell like a freshly plastered schoolroom.

He didn't seem to mind the casts. He lay in his crib, day after day, clicking his plaster legs together. He never smiled. At the end of two weeks he had grown so much that the flesh bulged over the top of the plaster, so I called the specialist. It would be OK to take off the casts, he said.

When Maggie came home that night, we filled the dishpan with warm water and dipped the baby's legs up and down in it until the plaster was soft enough to rip off, a chunk at a time. The water grew cloudy. While we were changing it, the baby got cold and began to scream.

"Oh darling, let's wait until tomorrow and have the specialist do it."

"There's water under the casts. If we stop now, he'll get pneumonia."

"But you're squeezing him. He's screaming."

"I'm not squeezing him. You try it."

"No, you. You do it so much better."

It took an hour but we got the casts off. Then we dried him and wrapped him up and gave him a bottle but he was so worn out he went to sleep without drinking it. Maggie was worn out too. She gave me a guilty kiss and said, "Oh darling, you're such a good mother compared to me, you make me ashamed."

For quite a while after that, Maggie tried to be a more perfect mother. She bought a book on the care and feeding of infants. She fed the baby in the middle of the night. She fawned over him. But it was too good to last. One night she called up and said, "Look, dove, will you take care of his royal highness tonight if I don't come home for dinner?"

She came in at one-thirty while I was putting a bottle on the stove.

"Playing with dolls?" she said, letting her coat slip to the floor.

"Somebody's got to do it."

"Don't be so goddam sensitive, darlin'." She went in the bedroom and struggled out of her clothes. When I came in with the bottle she was in bed. The baby had fallen to sleep so I picked him up and brushed the nipple back and forth across his gums until he opened his eyes. He spit out the nipple and started to howl. "What's the matter with you, you little bastard?" I said, stuffing the nipple back in his mouth.

"Put your dolls away and come to bed," grumbled Maggie. "He's not hungry."

"Did you hear what your mamma said? She comes home all lit up like a lighthouse and says a baby that's growing doesn't need to eat."

"If you won't let me sleep, I might as well read," said Maggie. She took a book off the bed table and turned a few pages. Then she shut the book and ran her hand over her eyes. "I'm sorry," she said. "Jolly took me to a show. I'm afraid I drank too much afterwards."

I didn't say anything. The baby's pants were wet so I laid him on the changing table and folded a fresh pad of diapers. "Hey, Maggie," I said, "come here quick."

"What's the matter?" she said, slipping on her house-coat.

"His legs were shaking a second ago."

"Are you sure? Look at the little precious. Why, he's smiling." He was. He was smiling up at Maggie with his wet gums as if there was a joke between them. "He looks just like his daddy when he smiles," she said.

"But he takes after his mother. I could have sworn he had the DT's a minute ago."

Maggie got mad. "Stop beating around the bush," she said. "If you think I drink too much, say so."

"For gosh sake, I never said you drank too much. All I said was he acted like he had the DT's a minute ago. I didn't mean anything by it."

"All right. Skip it. He's not shaking now. Here, let me

do that. Do you suppose if you fixed me a short Scotch it would help me sleep?"

I went in the kitchen and poured half a shot of Scotch in a glass, then I added some tap water and brought it to Maggie. "Promise me," she said, cradling the glass in both hands, "if I ever get too high, will you let me know? I love the stuff but I'm a little afraid of it. I never told you this before, but Daddy was a heavy drinker. You might say he died of it." She polished off the Scotch and handed me the glass. "I wish Daddy were here now. He would have loved little Hubert. Did you ever see such skin, with such lovely blue glints in it? He used to be so ugly and now he's so beautiful with that golden fringe."

"Fringe?"

"His bangs. Haven't you noticed?"

His hair was changing all right. There was still a patch of black in back with a bald spot in the middle like the comedian in a burlesque show, but it was gold in front, as pure as Maggie's and twice as finespun.

"He almost frightens me," said Maggie. "There's something positively mothlike about him. You don't suppose we'll wake up some night and hear him banging against the sides of his crib like that beautiful monster we brought home from Turkey Run in the shoebox?"

"He's not a moth," I said. "He's just a little boy by the name of Joe."

"His name is Hubert. We really ought to have the Belkes in to look at him soon. God, but he's a pathetic little bastard. I'm almost sold on him myself."

Two nights later the Belkes trooped over, Hubert, his sister Belle, and the dog Tiny. After a while Jolly dropped in. They sat around drinking Scotch while Maggie gave them a lecture on child care. I went to the movies. It was my first night off in two months.

If Maggie could have her friends in to look at the baby I figured I could have mine. I called Mr. Barney the next day. He promised to come out on his next free afternoon so I went out and bought a couple of cans of beer. I waited for him all afternoon but he never showed up. While I was standing at the kitchen window, drinking one of the cans of beer, Lily came out on the back porch of the big house to shake out a bathroom rug. I rapped on the window and motioned her to come on up. Lily had never seen the baby without Maggie around. It turned out she was dying to get a close look so we spread a blanket on the floor and laid little Joe down in the middle of it. He kicked his big feet and smiled up at us.

"He's a cute little monkey all right," said Lily.

"His mother thinks he looks more like a moth," I said. "Would you like a beer?"

While I was opening the can of beer, Joe began to shake and shudder all over without crying. "Maggie wouldn't believe me the first time that happened," I said. "What do you suppose it is?"

"It's a convulsion," said Lily. "You let me handle this, Mr. Flowers." She filled a dishpan with lukewarm water and carried it slopping into the living room. Then she peeled off the baby's shirt and swished him around in the water by his armpits until the shaking died down. She seemed to know what she was doing. "Best thing in the world for a convulsion," she said. "You got a towel?"

When I came out of the bathroom with the towel,

Maggie was standing at the top of the stairs, screaming, "What the hell are you doing to my baby?"

"He had a convulsion," I said.

"He'll get his death of cold. Give me that towel."

I handed her the towel. She spread the towel in her lap and began to pat the baby dry. Lily stood at the head of the stairs, looking sheepish, while the baby cooed up at Maggie.

"What made you think it was a convulsion?"

"We were playing with him on the floor, then he began trembling all over. It was like the other night," I said, "only worse."

"He probably got a chill from lying on the floor." Maggie looked at the carpet with the water splashed on it and at the beer cans under the sofa. "This place looks like a pigsty," she said.

"If the baby's all right, I'll be going," said Lily.

"Don't let me keep you," said Maggie.

When Lily was gone, I said, "You got no right to talk to my friends like that."

"You have peculiar tastes in friends, I must say. Did either of you think to call the doctor? I thought not. Tomorrow morning you're taking little Hubert down to Baggypants for a checkup."

I took Joe downtown the next morning. The doctor went over him from head to foot with his cold steel stethescope without finding anything wrong.

"He's in good shape but let me know if it happens again. Are you working yet, Mr. Flowers?"

"How the hell can I work?" I said. "Someone's got to take care of the baby."

"I was just asking," he said.

The following Sunday Maggie was changing the baby when he began to tremble again. It was the first time she had seen him do it so she looked it up in the baby book. "Just as I thought," she said. "That wasn't a convulsion. The book calls it trembling. It's quite common in young babies." All the same, she called the doctor and at two o'clock he drove up in his old Cadillac. Joe had had a nap and a bottle in the meantime and looked just as healthy as he did the morning I took him downtown for the checkup. He wasn't losing weight, the doctor said, that was the important thing. He said we could take him out in the buggy if we wrapped him up warm. So that afternoon we went parading down Hyde Park Boulevard with Tiny padding at our heels. Everyone stared at the fancy buggy and the big dog.

"Maybe we should try another doctor," I suggested.

"Baggypants knows his business, darling. All babies go through this sort of thing. Yes they do," she said, making clucking noises at little Joe.

"People are looking at you."

"Don't be so inhibited. Look at that. He's smiling. If little Hubert grows any more spiritual I'll become almost as mawkish about him as you."

"Then you could stay home and I could get a job for a change."

"No, doll. You make a splendid mother, but you're not much of a breadwinner. The quickest way for you to be one is to take up your dancing where you left off so you'll be ready when Brogsitter opens the club."

"What club?"

"Didn't I tell you? Jolly's getting the nightclub bug

again. He introduced me to his friend Brogsitter the other night. I made a big play for him and I think he liked it. At least he went so far as to make a couple of passes at me. Jolly thinks Hubert will be willing to go through with it this time. The old lady is so knotted up with neuralgia she's out of the picture for all practical purposes. Hubert's managing her affairs."

"Oh for God sake, do we have to go through all that again? If I spend all my time practicing, who'll take care of little Joe?"

"Lily," said Maggie. "And it's not Joe. It's Hubert."

"It's Joe," I said. "And I know Lily better than you do. I don't think she'd do it."

"Don't be absurd, darling. Jigs will do anything for money. I'll arrange it with Belle."

March came in like a lion that year. It went out like a lamb. On the last day of March I put the top of the buggy down and took Joe for a walk. We went down 47th Street, past Chloe's to the lake, which was calm as a bathtub. I lifted Joe out of the buggy and he stared at the lake and stared at it. When we got home he went to sleep without his bottle and slept until ten that night when I woke him up to feed him. He drank an ounce of milk, then shot the nipple out of his mouth and went back to sleep.

"I still think we should get another doctor," I said.

"Don't be ridiculous," said Maggie. "I wouldn't be at all surprised if he's getting ready to teethe. Naturally it's painful when the gums come in contact with a foreign object such as a nipple. That's what the book says. Did you phone that crazy dancing teacher yet?"

"I forgot all about it."

"Then call him tomorrow. Let's open another bottle of Scotch."

We sat up until midnight drinking Scotch. Joe never woke up.

"He's adjusting himself to a new feeding schedule," said Maggie at breakfast. "If you'd followed Baggypants' advice when I came home from the hospital, you'd have saved yourself a lot of sleep."

After she left I woke up Joe and changed him. He yapped a little when I stuck the bottle in his mouth, then fell to sleep. It was that way all day long. When Maggie got home I was walking around in circles.

"Stop acting as if you had a stick of dynamite on your hands," she said, unzipping her dress. "He's just teething."

"But he's breathing funny. Are you going out again?"

"Yes, but if it will make you feel any better, I'll run over to Belle's and call the doctor first."

"Tell him about the breathing," I said.

The doctor arrived in twenty minutes, a record time for him. Maggie had a horror of unshaded lamps and was annoyed when he took the shade off the bedlamp to get a better look at the baby. "He looks positively blue in that light," said Maggie. "What could possibly be the matter?"

"I'd like to take him to the hospital for a couple of days," said the doctor. "If there's anything wrong we'll find out what it is and set your mind at rest. Get him ready and I'll take you in my car." He went over to the big house to call the hospital.

"Oh Christ!" said Maggie. "That means I'll be late meeting Jolly. We're engaged in some furious plotting to bring Hubert and Brogsitter together. It would be a shame to spoil it."

"We have to get the baby fixed up first."

"Of course, darling. I'll be ready in five minutes." It took her twenty.

The doctor drove us to a children's hospital on Cottage Grove that looked like it was having trouble pulling through the depression. A nurse took Joe and told us to go to the office and sign him in. "I suppose they'll want money," said Maggie. "I just don't happen to have any." It didn't matter. They marked "No payment" after the baby's name and said I could come back in the morning and pay an advance on the bill. The doctor disappeared and we sat down to wait.

"I wish that damn fool would hurry," said Maggie. "He knows I have a date."

Finally the doctor came down. He said the baby seemed perfectly normal now and offered to drive Maggie downtown if she'd wait five minutes while he looked at another patient. After ten minutes Maggie got tired of waiting and called a cab. I stared at the worn linoleum until the doctor showed up and drove me home. While we were waiting for the light at 51st Street, I said, "What causes convulsions?"

"Any number of things. When there are minor defects—the feet in this case—there are sometimes other defects that don't show up until later. If the trouble is in the brain, we won't know until he's six months old at least."

"In the brain?"

"It's a possibility. I'm telling you this in confidence. I wouldn't mention it to Mrs. Flowers if I were you. She might worry."

175

There was nothing to do when I got home so I went to bed. I was still awake when Maggie staggered in at two A.M.

"I had a perfectly lousy evening," she said, peeling off her stockings and throwing them over the empty crib. "Brogsitter never showed up and Jolly got very, very drunk. Just between you and me, Jolly's beginning to bore me with his eternal cuteness. Did Baggypants drive you home?"

"Yes. On the way he told me what might be wrong with the baby. It might be his brain?"

"How could it be his brain? There's nothing the matter with little Hubert's brain. If you think we ought to call in another doctor, let's do it and to hell with the money. We'll borrow it somewhere. By the way," she said, taking some bills out of her purse, "I borrowed thirty dollars from Jolly when he was drunk. That ought to hold them at the hospital. You can take it over in the morning." She went in the closet and slipped on her nightgown. Then she pinned her hair on top of her head and began to cold-cream her face in the mirror.

"Why shouldn't there be something the matter with his brain?" I asked.

"Why should there be?"

"My mother died in Dunning," I said. "She died insane."

The cover of the cold-cream jar clattered to the floor.

"Oh darling, no! Why didn't you ever tell me?"

"I forgot about it, that's why. I didn't think about it for a long time, then tonight the doctor said there was a chance it might be the baby's brain and I remembered."

"I'd have gone through with an abortion if I'd known.

176

No," she said, picking up the cover of the cold cream jar. "It can't be anything like that. Let's not even think about it."

But it was all I could think about.

When I tried to pay them at the hospital the next morning, the cashier saw "No payment" after the baby's name and sent me to the social worker. They finally got it straightened out between them and the cashier apologized. There were so many charity cases these days she said. She was anxious to make it up to me so I asked if I could see the baby without waiting for visiting hours. She said she was sure it would be all right and gave me the room number. The elevator wasn't working so I walked up the stairs.

"You made good time," said the doctor. "I was speaking to Miss Belke's maid less than fifteen minutes ago. She said she'd give you the message when you got in."

"I've been downstairs all the time," I said. "What's going on?"

"We're not sure. The baby was in a coma when I arrived. It may be a clot on the brain. We've got him in an oxygen tent. I called Belke-Wiel's and got in touch with Mrs. Flowers. She should be here in twenty minutes. You can wait here if you want."

I had never seen an oxygen tent before. It was a square piece of canvas with a window in it that fitted over the white iron baby bed. Through the window you could see little Joe in a pair of diapers but no shirt. His eyes were shut and he didn't seem to be breathing at all. He looked more mothlike than ever. Finally I went downstairs and went outside and leaned against a No Parking sign where I could watch the Cottage Grove streetcars going by. In about ten minutes a cab pulled up and Maggie stepped out.

"Oh darling, what's this all about?"

"They've got him in an oxygen tent. He's in a coma."

"Is it that bad?"

"Nobody seems to know," I said.

We went upstairs. The intern asked Maggie if she would like to look at the baby. "I'd rather not," she said. When she pulled out a cigarette he frowned and pointed to a pair of French doors at the end of the corridor. The doors opened onto a small stone balcony above the car tracks. There was a wooden chair there but it was covered with soot so we smoked standing up. Neither of us said anything. When we finished, we went back and sat down on a bench in the hall where we could see one end of the oxygen tent through the door.

The intern had a stethoscope around his neck. He lifted the end of the tent and pressed Joe's leg with his finger.

"His foot moved," I whispered.

"The intern moved it, darling."

"Does that mean he's dead?"

"Of course not," said Maggie.

But he was.

The doctor came out. "I'm very sorry," he said. "If you'd like me to go through with a postmortem I will."

"You might as well," said Maggie. "What will that cost?"

"About fifteen dollars. I must say you're taking it very well."

"What did you expect us to do?" she said. "Roll on the floor?"

When we got outside she said, "Would you mind awfully, darling, if we had him cremated?"

"Why would we have to do that?"

"In the first place it's cheaper. In the second place we can avoid a ceremony. The Belkes will probably be horrified but you can't please everybody. After all, we can't expect them to pay for it."

"But how are we going to get him cremated?"

"You leave that to me," said Maggie.

We went in the closest drugstore and looked up undertakers in the Yellow Book. Maggie picked out the one with the biggest ad because she figured that would be the cheapest and we rode over on the Cottage Grove car. A man in a swallowtail coat and striped pants let us in like he was the keeper of a cathedral. "Do we have the remains?" he said in a solemn voice.

Maggie didn't bother to answer. She flashed the man the look she reserved for waitresses and said, "We'd like to get this over with as quickly as possible." The man nodded and ushered us into a plushy office with high-backed chairs and a big fern. Maggie did all the talking. We didn't care about a fine casket, she said. We didn't want any ceremony. When the man described the different kinds of robes she cut him short.

"The cheapest," she said.

"About the ashes—"

"Get rid of them."

"We can scatter them if you prefer."

"Scatter them then." The man wanted to know our

names. Then he wanted to know my occupation. "Is all this necessary?" said Maggie.

"I'm afraid it is, madam. Where is your husband employed?"

"He's unemployed," said Maggie. "I work at Belke-Wiel's. That should be sufficient." When she gave him our address, the man's face lit up.

"Isn't that the old Belke residence?"

"It is," said Maggie, taking a cigarette out of her purse. "Do you know the Belkes?"

"We prepared the late Mr. Belke's remains," said the man, whipping out a cigarette lighter. "They are a wonderful family."

"Indeed they are," said Maggie.

So they talked about old Mrs. Belke and Hubert and Belle. Even Tiny got dragged into it somehow. Before we left, the price had been reduced to thirty-five dollars—as a favor to the family.

If the garage seemed empty the night before, it seemed twice as empty when we got home. Maggie went around folding diapers and baby shirts. She made me take the crib apart so we could get it down the stairs.

"Why can't we leave it up a while?" I said. "I keep thinking of the way he used to stare at the stars in the wallpaper."

"It's the psychology of the thing, darling. Lily probably has some friends that can use it. If not, we'll give it to the Salvation Army with the rest of the stuff."

While I was taking down the crib, Lily came up the steps and said the doctor wanted to speak to me on the telephone. "It's about the postmortem," said Maggie. "I'll take it." She threw her coat over her shoulders and ran down the steps.

My stomach did a flip-flop. I had to sit down on the striped sofa. Lily stood in the middle of the room, staring at the floor. "I'm sorry I can't send any flowers," she said. "Miss Belke don't pay me enough. I never complained about it before but I figure you got enough to remember him by."

I didn't say anything.

"Miss Belke says you can borrow the Buick to go to the cemetery."

"There isn't going to be a funeral," I said.

Lily went away shocked. I sat there alone, wondering what the doctor could be talking to Maggie about all this time. But I knew. They would have cut the baby open by now. They would have found his brain all tangled up like a figure eight. I had to grind my teeth together to keep from saying out loud, "I don't care how I wind up. I didn't want him to wind up that way. He never did anything to anybody." Then everything came to a focus and Maggie was standing in front of me.

"Darling, aren't you listening? I don't think you've heard a word I said. Baggypants detected a slight murmur the day you took him down for his examination but it's quite common in infants and he didn't want to alarm us. It had nothing to do with his brain. It was his heart."

It was like somebody rolled a stone off my chest. I jumped up and ran in the bathroom and closed the door. I clenched my eyelids shut but the tears came through so I held my head over the sink and let them come. They ran down the drain like they would never stop. After a few minutes Maggie opened the door. I sat down on the edge of the bathtub and covered my face with my hands.

"Please don't," she said, taking my head in her arms and pressing it against her stomach. "I can't bear it when you cry."

"He was the only thing I ever owned," I said. Then it started all over again. Maggie led me in the other room and we sat down on the sofa.

"Oh darling, this is so stupid. Now straighten up. Enough is enough. Little Hubert or Joe or whatever you want to call him is dead. But you and I will go right on living, there's no doubt about it."

"How can I go on living?" I said. "There's a hole in my heart."

"There's a hole in my stomach. I could use a little Scotch. How about you?"

"There's no more soda," I said, blowing my nose.

"Then use tap water," said Maggie. "There's a way out of every predicament, darling. Don't you see?"

THIRTEEN

Maggie was always changing. She looked good in black but you couldn't tell if she was in mourning for the baby or if wearing black was just another one of her notions like mixing Scotch with tap water instead of soda. Myself, I didn't like things to change. After Joe died, I thought we would go on like we had before, just the two of us, but nothing was the same.

"What's come over you?" said Maggie one night. "Don't you love me any more? I'm not exactly a fool, darling. If you loved me, I'd know it. What are you thinking about now? Little Hubert?"

"No," I lied, staring at the shadows that the street lamp cast on the bedroom wallpaper. "I was thinking it's time I got my old job back."

"But you've already got a job. Your dancing. And you'd better get on with it soon because that lovely Mr. Brogsitter is all hot to open a club with Hubert's money. If it isn't a going concern by September it won't be Jolly's fault. Or mine either."

"I don't trust that Brogsitter," I said. "He sounds like a dirty toad getting ready to pounce."

"Never mind what he sounds like. By this time next year, if you're half as clever as I think you are, you'll be making twice as much money as me."

"We could use the money," I said. But by May the money problem solved itself. Instead of the monthly check for fifteen dollars from my grandmother's estate, a letter came from Mr. Denham, saying the house on Cullerton Street had been sold again and there was going to be a new mortgage on it held by a bank. If I would sign the attached papers I would get a cash settlement for balance due, etc. Two weeks later I got a check for $413 and a note from Mabel in purple ink, announcing that Mr. Denham and herself were retiring to California and she forgave me for everything.

"I don't know what that violet-scented whore means by forgiving you," said Maggie, "but I do know there's no excuse for not taking lessons again."

So I dug up my old teacher in the Auditorium Building and my shoes with the taps on them and began to develop a little speed and some new tricks. Mr. Barney's legs were giving out and his days at Alexander's were numbered but he came out whenever he had an afternoon off and helped me work out a couple of surefire routines. He borrowed a five-dollar bill each time but it was worth it.

It was surprising how soon little Joe began to fade once I got back to work. I almost forgot he ever existed—until the postcard came. It was addressed to Master Hubert Flowers.

Six months old! Congratulations. Please remind Mother and Father that now is the time to take you to your doctor for inoculation to protect you against diptheria and whooping cough and for vaccination against smallpox. Your mother can ask your doctor about these or telephone the public health nurse. With best wishes for a healthy, happy childhood.

COOK COUNTY HEALTH DEPARTMENT

There was something magic about that postcard. Each morning after Maggie had gone to work I took it out of the drawer where I kept it hidden and laid it on the kitchen table and read it over again. It was like Joe was still alive, floating around the Belke's backyard in his long white nightshirt in the summer sunshine, and only the county health department knew about it. One Sunday Maggie was looking for a handkerchief and came across the postcard in the dresser drawer. She brought it in the kitchen where I was making breakfast.

"Were you preserving this for some reason?"

"I was saving it to show you."

"Well, I've seen it now," she said, tearing it up. "Let's not have any more fetishes. When a thing like this goes on and on, it's bad for everyone concerned. I know how you feel, darling, but you can't bring him back with a penny postcard. He never had a future, poor little devil, but you've still got yours. There are things you've got to forget if you want to go on living."

It wasn't any good telling Maggie I didn't want to forget. But with the postcard gone, there was only the memory of Joe's big feet sticking out the end of the oxygen tent when he died and even that faded after a while.

The Club 92 1/2 is one of the things I will have to figure out someday when I take psychology. In August Mr. Brogsitter found a former machine shop on the Near North Side that he considered a good location for what Maggie called a really intimate little club. You had to go up an alley to get to it. They decided to call it Club 92 1/2 because that was the number of its address. Maggie showed it to me one night by the light of a candle. It was a small brick building full of old axles and grease cups. In one corner was a toilet falling into decay and across the back of the building was a narrow room with a dozen smashed-up slot machines spread out on the floor.

"What do you think of it, doll?"

I peeled some candle wax off my finger and said, "I think Brogsitter is taking everybody for a ride. What about the old lady?"

"But nobody can take Hubert for a ride, darling, and the old lady is much too wrapped up in her neuralgia to know what's going on in the world these days. It doesn't look like much now, but it will knock your eyes out when we get it fixed up. The bar will run the length of this wall. The band will be in that corner, four pieces. That's all we have room for. The platform goes here," she said, pacing off three steps in front of the imaginary band.

"How can I dance in a space like that?"

"That's your problem, darling. You leave the rest to Jolly and me."

Neither Maggie nor Jolly had much to say about what went into that place. Mr. Brogsitter picked the furnishings up at an auction so they had to make them do. They had trouble with the building codes, then with the unions. Then it turned out there wasn't room for a band. The floor show, as Maggie kept calling it up until the last minute, boiled down to a piano player, a singer called Linda who claimed she didn't have a last name, and me. Linda had been kicked off two radio stations already but she was going around with Mr. Brogsitter so she got the job.

Nobody seemed to know what I was supposed to do but for Maggie's sake I practiced my pants off, working up three routines, one of them with a hat, all of them with a line of patter. Whenever I thought up some decent comedy business I worked it in, nothing broad, a slight movement of the foot here, an extension of the elbow there. I rehearsed backward and forward in smaller and smaller spaces until I was on the edge of perfection. Then one night at the end of September, the Club 92 1/2 staged a preview. It was really a party for Jolly's and Brogsitter's friends. I got pretty high. So did Maggie.

When I woke up the next morning, Maggie was standing by the bed with a shot glass in one hand, looking fresh as a daisy. "Fix me an egg, doll. Have a shot of Scotch first."

I couldn't look liquor in the face but I got up and made breakfast. "You were marvelous last night," said Maggie, dabbing jam on a slice of toast. "Your dancing wasn't spectacular but you were damned funny when you talked. To hell with dancing. Comedy's your forte."

"If it's a fort, I better go hide in it," I said. "I don't even remember what I said. I was just drunk."

"Then stay drunk," said Maggie. "Tomorrow night you'll be lining them up in the alley. You'll be a sensation."

I didn't feel like a sensation. After Maggie left I went in the bathroom to look for aspirin. The apartment was two years old by then and beginning to look like what it was—a couple of rooms above an old stable. The bathroom was a mess. I was sure there was aspirin somewhere but I couldn't find it so I got dressed and walked over to the drugstore to buy some.

I suppose if things in life happen like they happen in the movies, the laundry truck coming down 47th Street would have squashed me into a pancake as I came out of the drugstore and I would have died with a smile on my lips and gone to heaven and joined little Joe. As it was, I had sense enough to spring for the curb when I heard the tires squeal. I made a quick recovery but not without banging the side of my ankle against the curb.

"Why don't you watch where you're going?" shouted the driver.

I couldn't say anything for a minute because of the pain. "I must have turned my ankle," I said finally. "It's all right now." I got up and walked home. When I took my shoe off I was surprised to see that my ankle was turning blue. The longer I watched it the bigger it got and the more tender to the touch. I put my shoe back on while I could still get it on, then I limped over to Drexel Boulevard and got on the bus.

Maggie got home before me that night. If I thought she would throw her arms around my neck and burst into tears when I came hobbling up the steps I was mistaken. She took one look at the crutches and at the cast sticking out the bottom of my pants leg and said, "What the hell did you do now?"

"Well, you never put the aspirin back where anyone can find it so I went out to buy some. A truck came along when I was crossing 47th Street. I made a jump for the curb and broke my ankle. The bone specialist put the cast on," I said, "the same one we had for little Joe."

Maggie glared at me a few seconds, then she went in the kitchen. I could hear the ice cubes tumbling into the sink and the cold water running as she mixed herself a drink. When she came out of the kitchen, she said, "It's too bad our Scotch is running low. You'll need a drink yourself before I'm through with you."

"I guess the closest I'll ever come to being on the stage is having my foot in a cast," I said. "Ha ha."

"Oh, stop playing the fool. If you'd ever taken psychology, you'd know that what happened to you today wasn't an accident. Ever since I married you, you've hated the idea of making anything of yourself. Finally the chance you've been waiting for all your life is handed to you on a silver platter and what do you do? You break your ankle. I'd feel sorry for you if it wasn't so late in the day."

"I don't care what the psychology book says. I couldn't help it. It all comes of making people do what they don't want to do in the first place. Like all those lessons I never really wanted to take. It was all a mistake."

Maggie looked out the window into the Belkes' backyard where it was dark and there was nothing to see.

"I'm beginning to think everything was a mistake," she said.

The Club 92 1/2 lasted two weeks. It closed the day the doctor cut the cast off my ankle and I went limping home on a foot full of pins and needles like Rip Van Winkle. Maggie went to the club with Jolly. She was dead sober when she got home.

"I've had another horrible evening," she said, peeling off her gloves. "If Brogsitter hadn't closed the place up, the police would have done it for him. Every queer within ten miles of the Near North Side was there. They chattered all through Linda's songs. She was furious but Brogsitter doesn't give a damn. He's already made a deal with some Wop to turn the place into a spaghetti joint. He doesn't stand to lose a cent. Neither does Jolly. They can afford to laugh it off but I can't. I've offended Hubert's business sense and it bothers the hell out of me. But the part that bothers me most about the whole business is you. You've let me down something terrible."

"Well, there's no use crying over spilt milk," I said. When I came out of the bathroom, Maggie was sitting up in bed reading a book.

"I just had an idea," I said. "If I can hobble around

tomorrow, I think I'll go downtown to Alexander's and get my old job back."

"Is that what you call an idea?" said Maggie without looking up.

Something about the way she said it got me mad. I grabbed the book out of her hands and threw it across the room.

"Stop reading and listen to me."

"Look here!" she said. "Just what do you have in mind?" Then I noticed for the first time that my right hand was drawn back as if I was going to smack her one. I was more surprised than Maggie was. I stared at my hand for a few seconds, then I let it drop.

"I never raised my hand against a woman before in my life," I said.

"Or anyone else for that matter. You're a mouse, darling."

"OK, so what if I am? I'm sorry. But I know how you feel about Alexander's. When I go downtown tomorrow I won't go near the place if you don't want me to."

"You do whatever you want. I'm moving out of this dump on Sunday."

"Moving!" I said. "Where are we moving to?"

"I'm the one that's moving. You can stay here if you like."

I refused to believe it. I climbed into bed and took Maggie in my arms. I kissed her, I laid my head against her chest, but it didn't make any difference.

"I thought you loved me," I said.

"I do," she said, stroking my hair. "It's the one honest thing about me."

"Then why should anything else matter?"

"I don't suppose it would if you really loved me. I don't blame you for feeling about me the way you do. I dress well. I make up respectably. But I'm not as young as I used to be."

"But I do love you," I blurted out.

"Oh Christ," she said, shoving me away, "there's no sense in talking like this. Do you want me to be brutally frank with you? I don't believe you're capable of loving anyone but yourself. And don't remind me of that damned baby. I know you loved him but it amounted to the same thing. He was helpless. He needed someone to dress him, to feed him, to clean up his messes, to put him to bed at night. He was you as you've always wanted to be. You didn't want a wife, darling. You wanted a mother."

Sunday afternoon we emptied drawers and closets and packed everything in suitcases. Maggie was going to move into an apartment on the Near North Side with her friend Erica. She had ordered a taxi for five o'clock. We tried to drink up the last bottle of Scotch before the taxi came but the taxi came late and we both got drunk. At least I did. When the taxi finally came, I said, "What would you have done the other night if I had hit you?"

"I'd have stayed," said Maggie. "Good-bye, darling." I kissed her good-bye. Then I finished the last of the Scotch and fell asleep with my head on the kitchen table.

FOURTEEN

The world had changed a lot since I left my job at Alexander's. The air had been full of talk of the depression then. Now the air was full of talk of war. There was even talk of the depression being over but it didn't take long to discover that there were still enough people out of work so you couldn't just walk into a place like Alexander's and expect the new manager to give you your old job back. Mr. Barney had taken to the horses and then to the bottle. Then he disappeared into the flophouses of West Madison Street, and the new manager wasn't much interested in employing any old friends of Mr. Barney's. What was left of my grandmother's inheritance was going fast so as soon as the cast came off my ankle I started pounding the pavements again. Nobody would give me a job. At twenty-three I was already a failure. There wasn't a friend I could turn to. As a matter of fact the only friends I could think of were Mr. and Mrs. Finkel. Seven years ago when I wanted my old job back, Mr. Finkel wouldn't give it to me. It was for my own good he said, but in seven years I had had enough of my own good to last a lifetime and was willing to give the Finkels another try.

Things change and they don't change. The big elm tree was still growing out of a hole in the sidewalk in front of the Wildwood Pharmacy. But the drugstore that had seemed so modern and up-to-date when it was new looked small and old-fashioned compared to the big chain store down the street with its windows full of cut-price toothpaste. The same hot fudge machine was on the marble counter with the dust collecting on its chromium top in the January sunshine, but a new druggist was sweeping the floor. His name was Seeley Johnson and he liked to talk. "Stick around," he said, leaning the pusher broom against the soda fountain. "The old man's gone to the bank. He'll be back in a minute." He stopped talking long enough to wait on a couple of schoolkids who barged in on their way home for lunch to buy licorice whips and artificial bananas. Then he rang four cents up on the register and said, "You got to hand it to Mr. Finkel. He's smart. How many drugstores do you see with penny candy counters these days? Kids like that will be getting married ten years from now and having kids of their own. They'll still come in here from force of habit. Oh, I won't say some of them won't sneak into Liggett's when they have a one-cent sale, I do it myself. But when it comes to prescriptions, people don't trust the chains like they do the Wildwood Pharmacy."

I picked up the broom and took a couple of sweeps with it. "The Finkels always liked kids," I said. "It's too bad they never had one of their own. I suppose they're too old now."

"Not to adopt one," said Seeley as Mr. Finkel walked in the door.

Mr. Finkel looked almost handsome in his old age. His hair was steel gray. "Who is this sweeping my floor?" he said, taking the broom from my hands. "Wait till Mamma hears of this."

"I was just dropping by," I said. "I better go now."

"You hear that, Seeley? An old friend is dropping by and he is too busy to stay for lunch. What are you catching? A train? Come upstairs to the apartment. Mamma will drop dead."

Mrs. Finkel was setting the table for lunch in the little dining nook whose windows looked into the branches of the elm. Instead of dropping dead, she looked at me and frowned.

"It's Charlie Flowers, Mamma. Aren't you glad?"

"Of course I'm glad. But he's too thin. What would you like to eat?"

"A cup of coffee will do," I said. It was just like old times. There were pickles and pumpernickel and corned beef, piles of it. I ate like a hog while the Finkels talked about the old drugstore on Wilton Avenue, about my grandmother and her boardinghouse and about the old neighborhood and how it had changed. "The Melody Gardens aren't what they used to be," said Mr. Finkel. "They use them for prizefights now."

"And wrestling," said Mrs. Finkel. "You're late, Riv. This is Charlie Flowers." While we were talking, the door had opened and a little girl had come in. Her head with its short black braids seemed too large for her thin neck. Her eyes were so deep you could look into them forever without striking bottom. She nodded and sat down at the table.

"She waits until the other children have gone," explained Mr. Finkel. "Then she comes home alone. The teacher says she can be very smart but she is afraid to talk." When Riv finished eating, Mrs. Finkel wiped her face and sent her back to school and Mr. Finkel said, "Sometimes I think we should thank God for Adolf Hitler because he sent us Riv."

"What a thing to say, Hyman!"

Mr. Finkel smiled and shrugged his shoulders. "I do not mean it," he said. "You know what the Nazis are doing to the Jews? It is not pretty the picture they paint in the papers, but it is true. Mamma's cousin in New York is Riv's uncle. He paid her passage over but he has three of his own. He wanted Mamma to find her a home. You know Mamma. She is too generous."

"When we saw her eyes we were not sorry," said Mrs. Finkel. "She was afraid of us at first but she is better now. I think she was not so afraid of you when she left. You are fond of children, no?"

"I ought to be," I said. "I had one of my own." They made me tell them all about it. When I got to the end Mr.

Finkel said softly, "That such a thing should happen to our Charlie! Sometimes I think we are too lucky."

"It was a terrible blow for the mother?" said Mrs. Finkel.

"She got over it," I said. "After the baby died we drifted apart. Now I'm looking for a job."

"I know of no jobs," said Mr. Finkel. "I am sorry because for a long time now I feel I owe you a job. Many years ago you wanted your old job back but I couldn't pay you what you were worth. A nice boy like Charlie, I thought, he can always get a job. Then things got worse and I would see grown men selling pencils and apples on the street corners and it would be on my conscience I turned you down. But now—what can I do? In the summer I put on a boy or two from Wildwood High, but you are not a boy. If you had finished school and gone to pharmacist college, then it would be different. Even so, what chance has a man with the chain stores closing in? You heard about Liggett's down the street? A drugstore they call it. They sell electric fans in summer, electric heaters in winter, electric percolators the year round. Do they pay their pharmacists what I pay Seeley Johnson? Do they get up in the middle of the night to fill your prescription when you are sick? No. They would sooner sell you hardware. They would sooner feed you breakfast, lunch, and dinner. Dinner!" snorted Mr. Finkel. "They will sell you something called a steak sandwich and you will eat it sitting on a stool, like in a bar."

"Always I am telling him," said Mrs. Finkel, "if your customers want a sandwich, sell them a sandwich."

"Mamma is as bad as the chains. Buy an icebox. Fill it

with hamburger, with corned beef. Then I should hire someone to make the sandwiches too thick."

"I used to be a counterman," I said. "At Alexander's downtown."

"So!" said Mrs. Finkel. "You have a lunch counter expert and you won't listen to reason."

"Business is bad enough," said Mr. Finkel, looking at me through his thick glasses. "It is better not to think about it."

"He will think about it," said Mrs. Finkel.

She was right. It took a little time to buy the coffee urn, the hamburger grill, and the high stools and have them installed but by February the lunch counter was a going concern.

The next two or three years were like a pool with all sorts of things going on around the top while I lay on the bottom holding my breath, only coming to the surface long enough to take a breath of air and see what was going on.

Seeley Johnson and his wife bought a house in Wildwood that spring and I moved into their vacant bedroom to help pay the mortgage. I could walk to work and had a lot of time on my hands but I didn't do much with it except sleep and go to the movies. Then one night that August the telephone in the drugstore rang. "It's for you," said Seeley. I went in the booth and closed the door. "Hello," I said.

"Hello, darling."

For months I had been waiting for the call that would tell me Maggie was dying of consumption in a cheap hotel on North Clark Street and I should come at once. The voice on the phone didn't sound like it was dying of consumption, or living in a cheap hotel either. "I had a devil of a time tracking you down," it said. "What have you been doing with yourself?"

"Right now I'm running a lunch counter for an old friend."

"How wonderful. Look darling, I hate to change the subject but I'm going to Paris in a few months. Hubert is sending me on business and I'd like to get a few legal details straightened out before I go. How about a divorce?"

"What would that cost?"

"As far as you're concerned, absolutely nothing. When the papers are served, accept them, but don't for God's sake show up for the proceedings. Desertion they call it. Have you any objections?"

"I can't think of any. Only—"

"Only what?"

"I don't know," I said and hung up.

A year later Finley and Dunlap's ran a series of ads in the paper to celebrate its Golden Jubilee. From Monday to Thursday the ads were screaming you should sit tight for the most important announcement in Chicago department store history. On Friday the important announcement was spread across a full page opposite the society column and Hints for Women. Belke-Wiel's was giving up their Michigan Boulevard store to open the Belke Salon on the seventh floor of Finley and Dunlap's. "Formal opening Friday evening at nine," it said in the lower right-hand corner. "Invitation only. Cocktails."

Friday night I arranged with Seeley Johnson to take over the sandwich counter so I could go downtown and see what the formal opening of the seventh floor of a department store looked like.

State Street was boiling with curiosity seekers by eight-thirty. There was a long canopy and a carpet reaching from the curb to Finley's front door. There was a bank of Hollywood floodlights across the street that lit up the old store like a movie set. There were doormen in livery to open the doors of the Lincolns and Cadillacs as they arrived and a special detail of policemen to hold back the crowd as the society people in their gold and silver slippers and black top hats trotted across the plum-colored carpet like racehorses on display. Maggie was already inside I guess, passing out cocktails on the seventh floor. Somehow I couldn't picture her insulting customers like she did in the old days—or walking out of Finley's with a calla lily in her hair to win a ten-dollar bet.

I didn't envy her. As far as I was concerned my own life was just as successful as Maggie's. And as I walked away from Finley's under the bright lights of State Street, I could picture my future life stretching out before me like an unbroken highway from Finkel's sandwich counter to the grave with not even the depression to stand in its way. For the war in Europe had begun the year before and the depression was officially over.

Mr. Finkel took to the war like a duck to water. After Poland fell, the war petered out for a while but the following spring Norway fell, then France, and Mr. Finkel rose up like the Wildwood Pharmacy was in danger of invasion. He bought a table radio and kept it in the back room so he could listen to the news. I couldn't see any point in getting excited but the next year Russia got itself invaded and all the men in Chicago had to register at their draft board so they could be called up to defend their country in the proper order. That shook me up a little. To make things worse, the owner of the grocery store across the street retired that summer and leased his vacant building to another cut-price drugstore. The Wildwood Pharmacy was so gloomy and empty that autumn you would have thought you were back in the depths of the depression. It didn't take much figuring to see that me and the lunch counter were so much extra baggage. All autumn I walked around in a sort of a daze, as my new life, which had once seemed so solid, crumbled and dissolved like a lump of sugar in a cup of hot tea. Then a letter came from the draft board in November telling me to report the second Monday in December for induction in the army and I came to my senses at last.

Now I knew enough about my own luck and had seen enough war movies to know that if this country ever did get mixed up in the war in Europe I would be the first to be found gassed in the middle of a field in France with a bayonet sticking out of my stomach. Under the circumstances I figured it might be wiser to volunteer in something safer than the army—like the navy or the Army Air Corps. I had until Monday to make up my mind so I went downtown Saturday to the big post office on Clark Street where you went to join the Air Corps, which is what they called the Air Force in the days before it broke off from the army and got a name of its own. The soldier in charge of the recruiting office was getting ready to close for the afternoon but he stayed open long enough to give me the works.

"The Air Corps is really on the beam," he said, jingling his keys. "There's no limit to the money you can make if you fly. You don't have to be a pilot either. Just volunteer for a bomber crew. But you got to act now or you'll wind up in the infantry and sure as you're standing here they'll send you to Louisiana to lie around in the mud on maneuvers."

"I'll think it over," I said, wondering if lying in the mud in Louisiana wasn't maybe safer than tossing loaded bombs out of an airplane.

"That's right. Think it over! I've seen too many guys walk out of here to think it over. By the time they made up their minds it was too late. What about your education? Do you have a degree?"

"I don't even have a temperature."

"Well, don't get discouraged. They're letting down the bars on bombardiers. All you have to have is a high school diploma." But when he found out I never went to high school he lost interest. "Why don't you come back Monday and talk it over with the lieutenant?" he said. "We're closing now."

I had quit work the day before and had nothing to do so I went to a bar on Wabash Avenue close to the North Shore station and had a couple of beers and wondered what to do next. The bar was already beginning to fill up with sailors on leave from the Great Lakes Naval Training Center, all trying to get tight quick for a big weekend in town. I asked the sandy-haired sailor on the stool next to mine if the navy had any education limit like the Air Corps. No he said, they took anybody. "Show up at the nearest recruiting station at nine A.M. Monday and the army can't touch you," he said. "You're as good as in."

I thanked him for the information and bought a round of beers. Then he bought a round of beers and I had to listen to his troubles. He had been waiting for a girl named Gladys since three o'clock but it didn't look like she was going to show up. Gladys was a blond. "I used· to know a blond," I said to keep the ball rolling. "She was very well educated for a blond, especially in psychology."

"I go for the sophisticated type. You got her number?"

"She works at Finley's," I said. "She sells dresses."

"You're drunk, Mac. You got a blond on the string who gets her clothes on a discount and has a couple of friends who are dying for a lay. Gladys isn't gonna show up. What are we waiting for? All you got to do is drop a nickel in the phone over there and we're fixed until Monday morning."

I wasn't drunk. I wasn't exactly sober either or I wouldn't have opened up to a stranger about Maggie like that, but after talking so big I was ashamed to back down. So I sat down in the telephone booth in a pool of stale cigar smoke and dialed Finley's while the sailor held the telephone book. When the operator answered I asked for the seventh floor. A ritzy female voice said, "Belke Salon."

"Miss Werner, please."

"Miss Werner is very busy. If you'll leave your name I'll tell her you called."

"Tell her Charlie called. Tell her I'm joining the navy. Tell her I called to say good-bye."

"Hold on," said the lady in a more human voice. "I'll see if I can locate Miss Werner for you. I have a brother in the navy. He's an ensign at Pensacola. You're not on your way to Florida by any chance?"

There was a sign above the coin box showing Uncle Sam with his finger to his lips. "I can't discuss troop movements," I said and opened the door a crack to get some air. The sailor stuck his head in.

"Hey Mac! Gladys showed up."

"Hello," said Maggie.

"It's me."

"So I gather. What do you want?"

"I'm joining the navy Monday. I called to say goodbye."

"That's very interesting but I don't believe a word of it. I'm very busy right now. If it's money you want, I'll mail you a check. I'd rather you didn't come up here."

"Who said anything about money? I was downtown celebrating and thought you'd let me buy you a drink."

"I could do with a drink."

"Hang up, Mac. Gladys has a friend on 95th Street. We're all fixed."

"Hello," said Maggie. "Are you still there?"

"Yes," I said, closing the door on the sailor's nose. "I'm in a bar on Wabash Avenue but it's full of sailors. How about meeting me at the Blackhawk? We had our first drink together in the poolroom there. This will be our last. I'll pay for it this time."

"You're not suggesting I meet you in a poolroom!"

"Of course not. I'll be in the downstairs bar."

"Very well. I'll be there in a few minutes." Then she

lowered her voice as if she didn't want to be overheard. "Order me a Scotch while you're waiting. Make it a double."

"Tap water or soda?"

"Neat," said Maggie. And she hung up.

The first thing you saw when you came down the steps to the basement grill under the Blackhawk was the sea of artificial poinsettias in tall black vases, one to a table. Waitresses were laying silver and smoothing the snowy tablecloths under the poinsettias, getting ready for the dinner-hour rush. It was that peculiar time on a late Saturday afternoon in December when it is just getting dark outside and Christmas shoppers are in a mood to relax over a cocktail or a glass of beer while they make up their minds whether to have dinner downtown or go home and fix it themselves. The small bar on the main floor of the Blackhawk was already crowded. The basement grill wasn't crowded yet but you had the feeling it soon would be.

I sat down in a booth next to the bar and ordered a beer for myself and a straight Scotch for Maggie. For thirty minutes I nursed the beer along, keeping one eye on the foot of the stairs where the shoppers came piling in with bright-colored Christmas boxes under their arms. It had been more than three years since I saw Maggie. I was just beginning to wonder if she had changed so much I had missed her, when she came down the steps. She stood there in front of the pine-paneled wall of the basement grill, staring around her in annoyance until she saw me, then she came over and sat down.

"Why didn't you say you'd be down here?" she said,

shoving the poinsettia to one side. "I've been waiting up-stairs for at least fifteen minutes."

"I said downstairs."

"Downstairs in reference to the poolroom, certainly. I didn't dream you'd be in the grill. This dive smells like a cellar."

"It is," I said.

"Everything OK?" said the waitress coming over.

"I told you to order me a double, darling."

The waitress took the shot glass back to the bar. "Make it a double, dahling," she said to the bartender. Maggie pretended not to notice the waitress was imitating her. "Now," she said, "what's this all about?"

"It's like I told you on the phone. I'm joining the navy. I wanted to say good-bye."

"Oh come now, you can't expect me to believe that." The waitress set a double shot of Scotch in front of Maggie. She took a sip and said, "This will have to be fast. Hubert's going to pick me up in a few minutes. If I'm not out in front by five-fifteen, he'll have to park."

"He can't park on Wabash Avenue."

"My dear, you'd be amazed where Hubert can park." She peeled off a glove and took another sip. "If this is really a farewell party, why don't you have a Scotch yourself? You've never really tasted Scotch until you've tried it straight. Drinking it straight preserves the smoky flavor. That's what Daddy used to say."

"Thanks, I'll stick to beer."

"Bottoms up," said Maggie. She peeled off her other glove and began to fumble in her purse. "It's lousy Scotch," she said. "I'll pay for it."

"No you won't," I said, signaling the waitress. "How about another?"

"I'd love it, if only to show my appreciation. I promised Hubert I'd only have one but what he doesn't know can't hurt him." Then she noticed me looking at the small circle of diamonds on her ring finger and said, "Do you like my ring? Hubert insists I wear it. We're married you know."

"Was that why you wanted a divorce? You told me you were going to Paris."

"But we fully intended to go to Paris. We were all packed when war was declared. Then nobody could go, but nobody. So Hubert took me to Rio instead. We flew all the way from Miami. Promise me, darling, if you ever go to Rio you'll fly." The waitress brought another double Scotch. Maggie made a point of letting it sit in front of her untouched for several seconds. Then she picked it up and took a sip.

"OK," I said. "I promise. As a matter of fact I was thinking of giving the Air Corps a fling before I decided to join the navy. Every once in a while I get the feeling I want to go out and drop bombs on people."

"You have delusions of grandeur, doll. The Air Corps's not for you. You'd be afraid of hurting someone. What made you switch to the navy?"

"The navy sounded more dangerous what with the submarines and everything. Speaking of the navy," I said, "down the hatch."

"Down the hatch," said Maggie. She polished off the Scotch and helped herself to a cigarette. Then she pulled a gold lighter out of her purse. I lit the cigarette for her and held the lighter in my hand a minute.

"I hate to sound like Mrs. O'Reilly," I said, "but you must be worth a lot of money by now."

"Don't be nasty," said Maggie, snatching the lighter out of my hand. "I had to work to get where I am. It wasn't an accident, my coming back to Finley's. I went back on my own terms, don't forget that. And don't think it was easy convincing a stuffy conservative like Hubert that an establishment like Belke -Wiel's could take over an entire floor in a department store without losing its identity. Belle thinks that's what killed the old lady. Maybe it did, but it worked. Most of my ideas do."

I ordered another Scotch while Maggie was talking and she calmed down. "How's the rest of the old gang?" I said. "How's Jolly?"

"Jolly's simply not speaking to us any more. He managed to patch up that business about the club but he never forgave Hubert for getting married."

"How's Belle?"

"The same as ever. She inherited part interest in the business when the old lady died so I have to be nice to her. Belle's the type that's willing to give you her right arm as long as she thinks it's charity, but just let her get the idea you're chiseling in on the family fortune and she treats you like dirt. It's so ridiculous. We all have to start somewhere. Just between you and me," she said, pushing the poinsettia further out of the way, "Belle's queer as a zebra. There was a time she could have gone for me in a big way if I'd been that kind."

"I always wondered how we got that garage apartment for fifteen dollars a month," I said.

"Why you louse!" shrieked Maggie.

"Ladies don't get drunk," I said. "They don't shout either."

"I don't care, darling. I think that was mean."

"Have another drink. It'll cheer you up."

"Suppose you think I can't hold it."

"Sure you can," I said. The next time the waitress passed the booth I raised one finger and she brought another Scotch. "Where were we?" said Maggie, taking a ladylike sip.

"You'd just taken over Finley's and raised everybody's salary."

"Don't be silly. Everyone's making loads of money right now. We lose help to the factories every week. You can't expect Finley's to compete with the war plants. As it was, we raised wages the first of the year and do you know what the bastards did to show their appreciation? They formed a union. Not a democratic one like we had. They sold themselves lock stock and barrel to the CIO. A bunch of long-haired radicals if you ask me. All they need is the beards. You know who's behind this superunion, just as hotheaded and stupid as ever? Your old friend Richard."

"Not him," I said.

"Yes him," said Maggie with a hiccup. "Pardon me. Back in a minute, darling."

She finished her fourth double Scotch and went weaving off between the tables in the direction of the ladies' room. The tables were really filling up now. There was a waiting line at the foot of the stairs and the headwaiter was eyeing our booth as if he was balancing the take from Maggie's double Scotches against dinner for four. I ordered another Scotch and another beer. When Maggie came back, I said, "Do you want to go? It's five-thirty."

"Should say not. Haven't had such fun in years."

"What about Hubert?"

"To hell with Hubert. He's probably wandering around upstairs. He wouldn't dream of looking for me down here." A paper boy came up to the booth and tried to sell us a paper. Maggie shooed him away and applied herself to the Scotch. "I get so bored with the news," she explained. "If it isn't Roosevelt, it's this silly business about the Japanese. If the President can whip us into a war with the Japs, we'll declare war on Germany too and spend the next few years fighting Hitler for the Russians and a handful of European Jews. The Germans and Russians can fight each other until they drop as far as I'm concerned, but just between you and me, doll, the Russians aren't going to last much longer."

"Last summer they weren't going to last six weeks."

"It's a miracle they've lasted six months. It's their psychology, darlin'. They're nothing but peasants."

"This is where I came in," I said. "I'll be back in a minute."

When I came out of the washroom I saw Maggie across the room before she saw me. There were faint circles under her eyes, the kind that show up sooner in blonds than in other women. It wasn't hard to picture what she would be like in another ten years, the type of woman she used to poke fun at because they wore girdles and rustled when they walked. When I sat down she said, "Why so serious, darlin'?"

"I was thinking about the time we drank bootleg beer in the poolroom upstairs. You had on the same kind of black dress. You wore your hair the same way. The only difference is there was a flower in it then," I said, "a big lily. You did it to win a bet."

"Not really! I couldn't afford to do a thing like that now. Snag that damn waitress. Miss!" she shouted as the waitress went sailing by with an armload of plates. I took the glass over to the bar. The bartender filled it and I carried it back to the table myself. "Thanks, darlin'. I know I shouldn't shout like that, but it's the only way you can get waited on in this lousy joint. Bottoms up! Let's talk about you for a while. How's the job coming?"

"You forget," I said, "I already quit to join the navy. It's a good thing I quit. Mr. Finkel's having a hard time making both ends meet."

"Finkel? That's Jewish, isn't it?"

"Does that make you better than him?"

"Don't lecture me on the Jews, darlin'. The clothing business is lousy with 'em. Sometimes I think Hitler was right."

"You folks want anything else?" said the waitress, standing over us with her pad. "Dinner? A sandwich?"

"I'll have another Scotch, please," said Maggie. "You see, darlin', I can be very polite when I'm with people I like. Oh thank you so much," she said when the waitress slopped the glass down in front of her. "Wanna know somethin', darlin'? You've changed. Never used to argue. Should get together more. Have some wonderful tiffs."

"Tiffs, my eye! You shouldn't make cracks about people you don't know. It's an insult to the Finkels. It's an insult to Riv."

"Who's Riv?"

"Mr. Finkel's daughter."

"Oh ho," said Maggie, wagging her finger. "In love with the boss's daughter! At long last I do believe I'm jealous."

"Nothing lasts long these days," I said. "You don't have to pretend to be jealous. I'm not getting married again, not to Riv anyway."

"Very sensible, darlin'. Innerracial marriage never work out. This Riv person wouldn't have you anyway. Jewish girls very particular, will say that for them."

"Riv can't afford to be particular," I said. "She's only nine."

"Damn your eyes, darlin'. Make a fool out of me again. Don't pull Maggie's leg. Not nice."

"Nobody's pulling your leg."

" 'Sall right, doll. Wanna hear a secret? Don't care a damn for Hubert. Not that way. Used to be mad about you. Trouble with you, you never gave a tinker's damn about me. All you cared about was that damn baby."

"You should know. You got all the psychology."

"Don't be spiteful, darlin'. 'Nother drink?"

"Another one of those and you won't be able to see for a week."

"Jus' one more, please. Love me, darlin'?"

"I did once," I said. "You were different then."

"No different," said Maggie, taking the poinsettia out of the vase and sticking the stem in her hair. "Look, darlin'." She giggled. The poinsettia bobbed up and down on its wire stem. "Wanna hear somethin' perfectly 'musin'? Hubert won' let me drink when he's not around. Thinks I can't hole my liquor. Now isn't that ridiculous? Where's that damn waitress?"

"Oh for God sake," I said. "Let's go."

"One more, darlin'."

"Well one more," I said. "One or two."

A wintry wind was whipping down Wabash Avenue. Hubert Belke was standing in front of the Blackhawk, staring at Marshall Field's Christmas windows across the street when Maggie lurched up the steps from the basement grill. He looked more like a melon than ever. Maggie staggered and caught his arm. " 'Lo, darlin'," she said. The poinsettia fell out. She put it back and the wind blew a strand of honey-colored hair over one eye. Two women passing by turned to stare. "Go t'hell," said Maggie. The women laughed.

Mr. Belke sized up the situation like a true businessman.

"Do I owe you anything?"

"I guess I owe you."

"For what?"

"For taking her off my hands," I said.

Hubert Belke turned his back. "Listen, Margaret," he said. "I'm parked in the alley by the library. Think you can make it?"

"Course I can. Bye, darlin'."

"Good-bye," I said, and the last I saw of Maggie she was rounding the corner of Randolph and Wabash on Hubert Belke's arm, a sodden blond with a flower in her hair and no place to go but home.

FIFTEEN

There were a few more good-byes to say before I joined the navy. Sunday I took the bus to the Belke house on the South Side and stood looking at the vacant apartment above the garage until Tiny, who was a very old dog now, began to bay at me from the back porch. From there I worked my way east to Mrs. O'Reilly's old house on Oakenwald, then to the bar on 47th Street where I proposed to Maggie. I had a couple of whiskey sours for old times' sake, then I walked over to the lake where you could see the buildings in the Loop and beyond them the Navy Pier. And

I said good-bye to them. An hour later I got off the streetcar in front of Finley and Dunlap's and walked over to Alexander's, where I had a sandwich and a cup of coffee, which I needed by then, because I had been having a glass of beer here and a shot there whenever I passed a bar. Half an hour later I got off the elevated at the Victoria, which was just another tired old movie house wired for sound. Finkel's old pharmacy was a poolroom now. I refreshed myself at the bar in the poolroom, then I followed the elevated tracks until I came to the cemetery. That was about as far back as I could go. I found the little hill next to the elevated tracks but it was getting dark by then and in that gray December light I couldn't find my mother's grave any more than I had ever been able to find my way back to that magic world of spotlights and fake barrel organs and monkey suits.

There was a bar next to the North Shore Station on Wilson Avenue a few blocks from the cemetery. It was full of sailors on their way back to the Great Lakes Naval Training Center. The radio was booming but it was mostly news so I didn't bother to listen. After a few beers I began to feel friendly so I went up to two sailors at the end of the bar and said, "One of my friends is at Great Lakes. Maybe you know him. He goes with a girl by the name of Gladys."

"What's his name?" said the tall sailor.

"I don't know," I said. "I only met him yesterday."

"Yesterday was a long time ago," said the short sailor.

"Well, don't give the ship up," I said. "I'm joining the navy in the morning." I dropped a nickel in the jukebox and pushed the button for "Anchors Aweigh." Then I pranced up and down the length of the bar a couple of times until the tall sailor shouted, "Hey you! Sit down. You oughtn't be playing the jukebox and dancing around like that when those guys in Honolulu are taking it from the Japs."

"How many times I got to tell you?" said the short sailor. "Pearl ain't Honolulu."

The bartender came over and unplugged the jukebox. The bar was closing he said, so I went in the doughnut shop next door and had a cup of black coffee. When I came out the two sailors were standing in the alley, talking to a Wilson Avenue bag with lipstick smeared all over her teeth. "Hurray for the navy," I shouted, throwing my arms around all three of them.

"Well, if it ain't the Jap spy from Harry's bar," said the tall sailor.

"Who did you think it was," I said, "the King of Siam?"

"Siam?" said the short sailor. "Ain't that in Japan?"

"Close enough," said the tall one. "Excuse us, Ma'am." The next thing I knew a cop was picking me up off the curb on Wilson Avenue where I was letting my nose bleed into the gutter. "Any other time I'd take you in," he said. "Go home and get your face fixed up." He helped me into a taxi and not long after dark I staggered into the Wildwood Pharmacy. There were no customers in the store but the radio was going full blast in the back room. Mr. Finkel reached me just in time to drag me around the soda fountain so I could be sick in the sink. He let the water run in the sink a while, then he took me in the back room and patched up my face.

"How did you manage to do this to yourself?" he said. "Couldn't you wait until you got in the army?"

216

"I was trying to avoid it by joining the navy but I changed my mind. Why don't you turn that damn radio off? It's nothing but news." Mr. Finkel clicked off the radio. The sudden silence made my head ache. "Can I have a Bromo?" I said. Mr. Finkel fixed me a Bromo and I drank it leaning against the soda fountain.

"You were right," he said, looking at me through his thick glasses. "It's nothing but news. It's like I was saying to Mamma. Always the worst news comes over the radio. Austria. Czechoslovakia. Poland. Norway. France. Russia. And now this."

"What's it all about?"

"While you were making up your mind to join the army, the Japs were bombing Pearl Harbor and getting us into the war."

"Who wants Pearl Harbor?" I said. "We still got Florida."

"Charlie, Charlie, why must you turn everything into a joke? Ever since you used to pound on the candy counter with your pennies in the store on Wilton Avenue, things have been changing. The country, the people, the world, Mamma, me, Riv, everyone but you. Why don't you grow up?"

"I'm twenty-six."

"You're six," said Mr. Finkel. He took a deep breath and let it out with a sigh. "I used to wonder what the army would be like for young men like you," he said. "What I think now is that for some of you it will be good and for some of you it will be bad but in the long run, for you, I would say it will be good. Good-bye, Charlie."

"Good-bye," I said.

There was one more good-bye to say. On my way to the army induction center the next morning I got off the streetcar at my grandmother's old stop.

The Melody Gardens seemed to have shrunk as much as the neighborhood. In the old days the wooden fence in back of the gardens seemed as high as the sky but on the gray morning after Pearl Harbor the fence seemed low enough to vault without a pole. It was weather-beaten and full of cracks. I looked through one of the cracks but there wasn't much to see. Weeds had grown up in the gravel paths. Old newspapers were blowing around between the bandstand and the trees. The Melody Gardens were out of business for good.

Finally I took my eye from the crack and started back to the streetcar stop. Halfway to the corner, I heard a streetcar coming. Then all at once I felt like Columbus setting out to seek his fortune and started to run. I was afraid I wouldn't be on time to join the army. But I was.